ADA HALPERIN

COOKING AND BAKING
FOR LOW FAT DIETS

*A selection of recipes compiled particularly for suffers
from coronary thrombosis and kindred ailments, using
ingredients free from animal fats and the whites of eggs
only and sunflower or corn oil*

BAILEY BROTHERS & SWINFEN LTD.
Folkestone

Published by Bailey Brothers & Swinfen Ltd.

© Ada Halperin 1970

First British Edition 1974

SBN 561 00208 8

Printed in Great Britain by
Clarke, Doble & Brendon, Ltd.,
Plymouth

CONTENTS

PREFACE

Just over a year ago, I suffered a coronary thrombosis and on being allowed to resume my normal household duties, I was faced with the problem of having to cook without eggs and fat (not to mention other dairy products) for myself and in the usual way for the rest of the household.

My husband insisted that what was good enough for me was good enough for him but that, in turn, posed the problem of providing nourishing and varied meals from the limited kinds of foods permitted to me.

The list of "untouchable" foods presented to me by my medical advisers, was truly formidable and the thought of never being able to satisfy my liking for cakes and biscuits was most depressing, but the list did say that sunflower or corn oil could be used, as also the whites of eggs, skimmed milk and skim milk cheese. On experimenting, I found it amazingly simple not only to keep to my diet, but also to provide varied meals for the household and for visitors, who are surprised when told that they are eating fat-free cooking.

This book is the result of my experiments and has been compiled for the housewife who has the average knowledge of cooking but is forced to adapt herself to the demands of a fat and egg-free diet. However, I have tried to give the recipes in such a way as to make them simple enough for the inexperienced cook to follow. All the recipes have been tried and tested and all the measuring has been done with standard equipment, consisting of an 8 oz. measuring cup and a set of graded measuring spoons. All measurements are level, unless otherwise stipulated.

As mentioned, the book is particularly for sufferers from coronary thrombosis and kindred ailments, but as sufferers from liver complaints also have to follow a fat and egg-free diet, I hope that they, too, will find the recipes useful. Incidentally, my husband has lost weight since following my diet and says he has never felt better and people wishing to reduce might also find this book of interest.

The diet consists of all fruits, vegetables and cereals. It includes bread, toast, oatmeal, maize meal, jams, tea and coffee. Egg white, lean meat and fish may be eaten in reasonable amounts. Poultry is also allowed but the lean and dry portions are to be preferred. Fish is probably better than meat. Salt and pepper, tomato sauce, pickles, mustard, Worcester sauce are all allowed. Brown or whole-wheat bread is preferable to white. Maize meal and oatmeal are better than refined products. Avocado pears, olives, peanut butter and all nuts are allowed (only Coconut should be avoided). Alcohol in small amounts, Bovril, Oxo, Vitamite, Marmite and Vegimite are all allowed.

The need for this book is shown by the increased incidence of coronary thrombosis in many parts of the world. This book will, I hope, be a means of in some cases averting such attacks and in others alleviating the results.

In my own case, I am convinced that this diet has so improved my condition that I have no fear of a recurrence.

THE FOLLOWING FOODS ARE NOT ALLOWED

Meats	*Dairy Products*	*Soups*
Bacon	Milk (except Skimmed Milk)	All tinned
Hamburger	Condensed Milk	soups unless
Pork or Ham	Cream	certified fat-
Sausage	Ice Cream	free.
Frankfurter	Butter, Margarine, Fat or Lard	
Tongue	Cheese (except Skim Milk Cheese)	
Polony	Yolk of Egg	

Every housewife will have her own special likes and dislikes as far as soups are concerned and providing the soup is prepared in the way I suggest, it will be suitable for a fat-free diet. I prefer making soup with knuckle of veal, which has little or no fat and when buying knuckle of veal, I ask my butcher to chop it into convenient pieces, as a whole knuckle would be too much for one pot of soup.

All soups should be made the day before using and left to get cold, when all fat will come to the surface and can easily be removed. If however, you are in a hurry, make the soup and, when ready, drop in two or three ice cubes and cool in the refrigerator so that the fat will come to the surface quickly.

As an alternative to the more usual soups, I have given a Chilean Fish Soup recipe which I recommend as being delicious.

✱ CHICKEN SOUP

1 Chicken (2½-3 lb.)	1 Onion
2 Grated Carrots	Chopped Parsley
2 Grated Turnips	Salt and Pepper
2 Bayleaves (optional)	4-6 Peppercorns (optional)

Method: Wash and clean chicken well and remove as much fat as possible. Season well with salt and pepper.

Put into saucepan, three-quarters full of water, together with the giblets, onion, carrots, parsley and turnips.

Boil until chicken is tender.

Remove chicken, which can be served as boiled chicken or browned in the oven.

Allow giblets and vegetables to boil gently for a further two hours. Strain and allow soup to get cold.

When the soup is cold, the fat will rise to the top and can easily be skimmed off. Reheat soup and serve with the giblets and croutons.

Croutons: Cubes of bread, fried in very little oil until golden brown and crisp.

5 or 6 Large Beetroots	1 Onion
1 Egg White	½ Teaspoon Salt
¾ Teaspoon Tartaric Acid or Lemon Juice (approximately)	2 Tablespoons Sugar Cold Water

Method: Peel beetroot and grate coarsely, put in large saucepan with 10 cups of cold water and onion. Boil until beetroots are soft (approximately 1 hour).

Beat egg white in a basin and add 4 cups of the soup gradually. Pour back into soup.

Add salt, tartaric acid, sugar. The mixture must have a sweet-sour taste.

Boil for a further 5 minutes, remove from stove and leave to cool.

Can be served strained or unstrained, hot or chilled. If served cold, add a little skimmed milk, skim milk cheese and a hot boiled potato in each plate.

✱ CREAM OF TOMATO SOUP

2 lb. Tomatoes	1 Carrot (grated)
1 Onion, sliced	1 Tablespoon Sugar (optional)
1 Teaspoon Salt	¼ Teaspoon Pepper
1¼ Cups Skimmed Milk	1 Tablespoon Cornflour
1 Heaped Tablespoon Tomato Puree	

Method: Boil carrot and onion in a little water (about 2 cups). Slice tomatoes and when carrot and onion are soft, add tomatoes, salt, pepper and sugar and 2 cups hot water.

When tomatoes are soft and pulpy, rub through strainer.

Replace on stove, add tomato puree and 1 cup milk.

Bring to boil and thicken with cornflour dissolved in ¼ cup of the milk. Stir, and let boil for a further 5 minutes. If not creamy enough, a little more cornflour can be added, as also more seasoning, if required. Strain.

✶ TOMATO SOUP

2 lb. Tomatoes, sliced	1 Large Onion, sliced
1 Carrot (grated)	1 Turnip (grated)
Handful Parsley	1 Bayleaf
4 Peppercorns	Stock or Water
3 Teaspoons Sugar (optional)	1 Tablespoon Cornflour
Sunflower or Corn Oil	
(2 tablespoons)	

Method: Heat oil in large saucepan and fry onions until slightly brown. Add tomatoes and leave for 5 minutes, or until same forms plenty of liquid.

Pour in stock or water to half fill saucepan, add carrot, turnip, parsley, bayleaf, peppercorns. Cover pot and let same boil slowly for 30 minutes or until vegetables are soft. Rub through strainer, pour back into pot and bring to boil.

Stir in cornflour, dissolved in $\frac{1}{4}$ cup water if soup is not thick enough. Add salt, pepper (and a little sugar, if required) to taste and let same boil for a further 5 minutes. Serve with toast cut into small squares.

✶ SPLIT PEA SOUP

Portion of Knuckle of Veal	1 Onion, grated
1-1$\frac{1}{2}$Cups Split Peas (depending on	1 Large Potato, grated
size of saucepan)	2 Turnips, grated
2 Large Carrots, grated	Salt and Pepper
A little cut-up Celery and Parsley	

Method: Put meat and vegetables into a large saucepan, three-quarters full of water. Add salt and pepper. Cover saucepan and boil for 30 minutes. Remove scum. Turn down heat and let soup boil gently for 2-2$\frac{1}{2}$ hours, or until soup thickens. More water can be added if necessary.

✶ BEAN SOUP

The same method is used for bean soup as for Split Pea Soup.

✶ CREAM OF MUSHROOM SOUP

1 Tablespoon Sunflower or
   Corn Oil
1 Pint Skimmed Milk
   Juice and Mushrooms of one 10 oz.
    tin Mushrooms

2 Tablespoons Flour
1 Cup Water
   Salt and Pepper
   Dash of Paprika.

Method: Heat oil and stir in the flour gradually. Add milk, water and mushroom juice and boil until mixture thickens, stirring constantly. Add mushrooms, thinly sliced, paprika, salt and pepper to taste. Simmer for a further 10-15 minutes.
   If too thick, more water or milk can be added.

✶ CREAM OF ASPARAGUS SOUP

The same method is used as for Cream of Mushroom.

✶ VEGETABLE SOUP

   Portion of Knuckle of Veal
2 Grated Turnips
   Handful Parsley
   Celery
1 Large Tomato, peeled and sliced

2 Grated Carrots
1 Large Onion (grated)
1 Large Potato (sliced)
   Salt and Pepper

Method: Place meat and vegetables in large pot, three-quarters full of water. Season with salt and pepper to taste. Bring to boiling point and let same boil for a minute or two, removing scum. Cover, and simmer for 2-3 hours.

✶ BARLEY SOUP

1 Cup Barley, washed
1 Large Onion (whole)
1 Large Tomato, skinned and
   cut up
   A little cut-up Parsley

   Portion of Knuckle of Veal
2 Carrots, grated
1 Large Potato, grated
   Salt and Pepper
1 Oxo Cube (optional)

Method: Place meat, vegetables and barley in large saucepan, three-quarters full of water. Add salt and pepper.

Cover and boil for half an hour, remove scum. Turn down heat and let same boil gently for 2½-3 hours or until barley gets soft and soup thickens.

More water may be added if necessary. An Oxo cube may be added to give soup good colour and flavour.

* CHILEAN FISH SOUP

1 Cup Sunflower or Corn Oil
2 Cloves Garlic, minced
3 lb. Fish, cut into 1 inch pieces (skinned and filleted)
2 Teaspoons Salt
4 Potatoes, cubed
4 Tomatoes peeled and sliced

4 Onions, chopped
1 Teaspoon Marjoram
6 Cups Water
½ Teaspoon Pepper
1 Cup Sherry
4 Tablespoons chopped Parsley (optional)

Method: Heat oil in saucepan, add the onions and garlic and simmer for 15 minutes, stirring frequently. Add marjoram, fish, water, salt and pepper.

Cover, and cook over medium heat for 30 minutes. Add the potatoes and pour in the sherry. Cover again and cook over medium heat for a further 20 minutes. Add the tomatoes and cook for a further 15 minutes. Serve hot. Sprinkle chopped parsley over each serving, if desired.

* FRIED NOODLES

1 Egg White
Pinch Salt

3 Tablespoons cold Water
1 Cup sifted Flour

Method: Slightly beat 1 egg white with 3 tablespoons cold water and pinch of salt. Gradually add 1 cup or more sifted flour to make a firm and dry dough, that does not stick to the mixing bowl.

13

Knead well and roll out very thinly on floured board. Cut into ½ inch squares.

Fry in deep hot oil until slightly golden brown. Remove onto brown paper to drain.

When cold, place in a large screw top bottle and close firmly. Use as required in chicken or other clear soup.

FISH

All fish should be washed well before using and in the case of fried fish, it should be dried thoroughly before seasoning.

✳ FRIED FISH

Wash fish well. Season with salt and pepper. Dip in flour and deep fry in hot Sunflower or Corn Oil until golden brown.

✳ OVENFRIED FISH

Sole, or filleted White Fish
Breadcrumbs

Salt and Pepper
Sunflower or Corn Oil

Method: Wash and season fish and if using white fish, cut into thin slices. Roll in breadcrumbs and place on an oiled baking sheet, or shallow casserole dish and sprinkle a little oil on top.
Bake for 10 minutes in 500° oven.

✳ PICKLED FISH

$1\frac{1}{2}$ Cups Vinegar
3 Bayleaves
   About 2 Tablespoons Sugar
     (to taste)
3 Large Onions
   Cold Fried Fish

$1\frac{1}{2}$ Cups Water
36-40 Peppercorns
   About 1 Teaspoon Curry
     Powder (depending on
     strength)
$2\frac{1}{2}$ Teaspoons Cornflour

Method: Bring vinegar, water, bayleaves, peppercorns and sugar to near boiling point. Add curry powder.
Slice onions and add to mixture and boil for further 5 minutes.
Thicken with cornflour dissolved in $\frac{1}{4}$ cup cold water.
Remove pot from stove and leave to cool, then pour over fish, which has been placed in a deep dish.

* BOILED FISH

2 lb. Cod or any firm White Fish   Salt and Pepper
4 peppercorns   1 Bayleaf

Method: Fillet fish and cut into serving pieces. Add salt and
pepper. Place in saucepan which is a quarter full of boiling water.
Add bayleaf and peppercorns. Boil at medium heat until fish is
soft.
     Serve with white sauce. (See Sauces.)

* ASPARAGUS FISH

1½ lb. Cod or other firm   1 Tomato, sliced
     fish, sliced thinly   Salt and Pepper
1 Onion, sliced   3 Teaspoons Cornflour, or Flour
1 Tin Asparagus tips   Pinch of Thyme (optional)
     Sunflower or Corn Oil

Method: Line oiled ovenwear dish with onions and tomatoes.
Top same with the fish which has already been seasoned with
salt and pepper.
     Make sauce as follows:
     Dissolve cornflour in ¼ cup cold water and mix with the juice
of the asparagus, add the thyme.
     Cut up asparagus into 1 inch pieces and add to sauce.
     Pour mixture over fish and bake in oven 350-400° for 1 hour,
or until fish is soft.

* GRILLED SOLES

4 Soles (skinned)   Salt and Pepper
     Chopped Peanuts   Sunflower or Corn Oil

Method: Season fish with salt and pepper, brush on both sides
with oil. Grill under broiler in oven.
     When soft, remove from oven, sprinkle chopped nuts over
same and return to oven for 2-3 minutes. Serve hot.

✴ STEAMED FISH

1 lb. Fish	Salt and Pepper
1 Onion, sliced	3 Peppercorns
1 Bayleaf (optional)	Juice of 1 Lemon

Method: Season fish with salt and pepper, squeeze a little lemon juice over same. Place in double saucepan with peppercorns, bayleaf and onion.

Steam fish for 30 minutes, or until soft.

Can be served with a sauce to make it more interesting. (See Sauces.)

✴ BAKED ROLLED SOLE

2 or 3 Soles, filleted	Salt and Pepper
¼ Cup cold Water	

Method: Season fish with salt and pepper. Roll fillets and secure with toothpicks. Place in casserole dish with water. Cover, and bake in oven (400°) for 30 minutes, or until fish is soft.

If desired, the above can be served with mushroom sauce, made as follows:

Mix mushroom juice of a 10 oz. tin mushrooms with 2 teaspoons cornflour. Pour into pan and bring to the boil. Then add mushrooms and continue boiling for a further 2 minutes. Pour this mixture over the baked fish and leave in oven for a further 5 minutes.

✴ BAKED FISH AND MUSHROOMS

2 lb. Cod or other firm White Fish, filleted and sliced	Sunflower or Corn Oil
	Salt and Pepper
	½ lb. Fresh Mushrooms, sliced
1 Egg White	½ Cup White Wine
Breadcrumbs	Lemon Juice
Water	Handful Chopped Parsley
2 Tablespoons Flour	

B   17

Method: Season fish with salt and pepper. Mix egg white with 1 tablespoon water and slightly beat. Dip fish in the egg white and then into breadcrumbs and place same in oiled shallow ovenproof dish. Sprinkle 1 or 2 tablespoons oil over top of fish and bake at 350-400° for 30 minutes, or until fish is soft.

Now prepare mushrooms. Wash same well and squeeze on lemon juice.

Cover bottom of frying pan with oil and heat well. Then turn heat down and add the sliced mushrooms, parsley and salt and pepper. Stir, then cover pan and cook for 10 minutes, or until mushrooms are soft. Then sprinkle with flour and mix.

Add $\frac{1}{2}$ cup water and wine and mix well. Allow to boil for a further 5 minutes.

When fish is soft, pour mushroom mixture over, turn down oven to 200° and leave for further 10-15 minutes.

✱ BAKED FISH WITH WINE AND MUSHROOMS

2 lb. Filleted and thinly sliced fish
2 Medium Tomatoes (skinned)
1 Tin Button Mushrooms
  Salt and Pepper
2 Bayleaves
  Pinch of Thyme
2 Teaspoons Cornflour (rounded)

1 Medium Onion
$\frac{1}{2}$ Cup White Wine
  Sunflower or Corn Oil
  Breadcrumbs
4 Peppercorns
$\frac{1}{2}$ Teaspoon Sugar

Method: Oil ovenproof dish well. Line with 1 skinned and sliced tomato. Season fish with salt and pepper and dip into breadcrumbs.

Put fish on top of tomatoes and sprinkle with 1 dessertspoon oil. Place in oven (400°) for about 20 minutes or until fish is fairly soft.

Prepare sauce as follows:

Fry sliced onion and the other skinned tomato in 1 tablespoon hot oil, together with pinch of thyme, bayleaves and peppercorns for 5 minutes, then add 1 cup mushroom juice, wine and sugar and let same simmer for 10 minutes.

Dissolve cornflour in $\frac{1}{4}$ cup cold water and add to sauce to thicken.

Remove peppercorns and bayleaves. Add mushrooms and pour over the baked fish.

Cover dish, put back into oven for about 5 minutes, turn down heat to 200° and leave for further 10 minutes.

✷ FISH IN MUSHROOMS

2 lb. filleted and skinned Cod
  (when buying the fish, keep the
  middle bone)
1 10 oz. tin Button Mushrooms
  Salt
  Tablespoon Sherry

½ Cup Skimmed Milk
1 Small Onion
½ Teaspoon dry Mustard
1 Tablespoon Cornflour
  Dash Cayenne Pepper
  Water

Method: Boil fish bones in about 2 cups water with salt, pepper and sliced onion for about 15 minutes. Leave to cool. Strain off ½ cup of the stock and discard the rest. Add the juice and mushrooms, ½ cup milk, cayenne pepper, salt, mustard, sherry and cornflour.

Return to stove and bring to boil, stirring constantly.

If sauce is too thin, add a little more cornflour, dissolved in very little water.

Place fillets of fish in an oiled ovenproof dish and pour boiling sauce over fish. Cover with lid and bake in moderate oven (350°) for about 20 to 30 minutes, or until fish is soft.

✷ BAKED FISH IN ANCHOVY SAUCE

1½ lb. Cod or other firm
  fish
2 Teaspoons Anchovy Sauce
¼ Teaspoon Pepper
1 Tablespoon Tomato
  Puree

1 Cup Skimmed Milk
1 Sliced Onion
¼ Cup Crushed Cornflakes
1 Full Teaspoon Cornflour or
  Flour

Method: Wash and bone fish and cut into thin fillets.

Oil ovenproof dish, line with sliced onion. Cover with fish then pour over sauce, made as follows:

Mix skimmed milk, cornflour or flour, cornflakes, anchovy sauce, tomato puree and pepper. Mix well.

Put into pre-heated oven (400°) for 40 minutes or until fish is soft.

* BAKED FISH WITH BREADCRUMBS

1 lb. Cod, or any firm fish	Salt and Pepper
Juice of 1 Lemon	1 Tomato, peeled
2 Tablespoons Tomato Sauce	Breadcrumbs
1 Onion, sliced	2 Bayleaves, 6 Peppercorns

Method: Boil fish with bayleaves and peppercorns. When soft, flake and bone fish.

Add some of the stock in which fish was boiled, tomato sauce, lemon juice, salt and pepper to taste.

Oil shallow ovenware dish and line with sliced tomato and onion. Add fish mixture and cover with breadcrumbs.

Bake in oven at 400° for 30-40 minutes, until top is lightly brown.

* LEMON BAKED FISH STEAKS

1 lb. Fish, cut into steaks	1 Lemon, peeled and sliced
⅛ Cup Sunflower or Corn Oil	Salt and Pepper

Method: Season fish with salt and pepper. Place in a shallow ovenproof dish with a slice of lemon on each piece. Pour oil over same and bake for about 20 minutes in moderate oven (350°).

* BAKED FISH FILLETS IN ORANGE

1 lb. Fish	Juice of 1 Orange
1 Teaspoon grated Onion	2 Tablespoons Sunflower or
Salt and Pepper	Corn Oil

Method: Wash and bone fish. Cut into fillets. Season with salt and pepper.

Mix orange juice, onion and oil.

Dip each fillet into mixture and place on an oiled shallow ovenproof dish. Pour rest of mixture over fish.

Bake in a moderate hot oven (375°) for about 30 minutes, or until fish is soft.

✱ BAKED FISH WITH TOMATO

2 lb. Fish	Salt and Pepper
Sunflower or Corn Oil	2 Onions
2 Tomatoes	Skim Milk Cheese

Method: Boil fish and when soft, flake and bone carefully and season to taste.

Oil ovenware dish, put in layers of sliced onion, tomatoes and fish, ending with sliced tomatoes.

Pour over white sauce and sprinkle with white skim milk cheese and bake in moderate oven for about 30 minutes.

White Sauce:

1 Dessertspoon Cornflour	1 Cup Skimmed Milk
1 Tablespoon Lemon Juice	1 Teaspoon Grated Lemon Rind

Dissolve cornflour in $\frac{1}{4}$ cup milk, mix to a paste. Add balance of milk, lemon juice and lemon rind. Pour into pan and heat and throw over fish as abovementioned.

✱ BAKED HADDOCK

1 lb. Haddock	1 Cup Skimmed Milk
1 Onion, sliced	3 Teaspoons cornflour
1 Tomato, sliced	$\frac{1}{4}$ Teaspoon Pepper
$\frac{1}{2}$ lb. Potatoes, sliced into rounds	

21

Method: Wash haddock well and cut into slices. Oil ovenproof dish and line with layers of onion and tomato, potatoes and fish.

Make a white sauce as follows:

Dissolve cornflour in $\frac{1}{4}$ cup of milk, and add to balance of milk. Add pepper and mix well. Pour this over fish and bake at 350-400° for 45 minutes, or until potatoes and haddock are soft.

✳ FISH CAKES (A)

1 lb. Boiled Fish
$\frac{1}{2}$ lb. Boiled Potatoes
1 Teaspoon finely cut Parsley
   (optional)

Salt and Pepper
1 Tablespoon Sunflower or
   Corn Oil

Method: Mash potatoes and mix with a little hot milk and oil until creamy. Stir in flaked fish, season with salt and pepper and form into flat cakes with lightly floured hands.

Fry the cakes in about 3-4 tablespoons hot oil, until light brown on both sides.

✳ FISH CAKES (B)

1 lb. White Fish
$\frac{1}{2}$ Cup Oatmeal*
1 Egg White, unbeaten
$1\frac{1}{2}$ Cups cold water

1 Medium Onion
Salt and Pepper
Sunflower or Corn Oil

Method: Mince fish together with onion. Add egg white, oatmeal, cold water, gradually mixing well all the time. Then add salt and pepper to taste.

Chill in refrigerator for 1 hour or more.

Make into round balls and fry in hot oil.

Makes about 20 fish cakes.

These fish cakes can also be made into very small balls and used as cocktail savouries.

* A 1 inch thick slice of bread which has been soaked in cold water can be used instead of the oatmeal. Less water should then be used and the fish balls can be fried straightaway.

✱ BREADLESS FILLETED FISH

2 lb. Cod or other White Fish
1 Egg White
  Salt and Pepper

2 Medium sized Onions
2 Medium sized Carrots
1 Cup cold Water

Method: Fillet and skin fish carefully. Place bones and skin of fish in a large pot with water. Add salt to taste.

Add 1 onion, 1 carrot, which have been cut into rounds and bring to the boil.

In the meantime, mince together filleted fish, the other onion and carrot. Mix in the egg white, then gradually add water, beating all the time. Lastly add salt and pepper to taste.

Form into balls and place in pot with the boiling sauce.

Let same boil for another 15 minutes, then turn down heat and let simmer for 1 hour.

Take out fish balls and carrots, strain the sauce and pour over the fish balls.

Can be eaten hot or cold.

✱ PILCHARD RISSOLES IN TOMATO SAUCE

1 Tin Pilchards in Tomato Sauce
  Juice of $\frac{1}{2}$ a Lemon
1 Teaspoon Tomato Puree
  Pinch Salt, Pepper, Paprika
  Sunflower or Corn Oil

1 Slice Soaked Bread
1 Egg White
$\frac{1}{2}$ Cup Skimmed Milk
1 Teaspoon Cornflour
  Flour

Method: Mash pilchards with a little of its tomato juice, add salt, pepper, paprika and part of the lemon juice and egg white.

Make into rissoles and dredge in flour. Fry in hot oil.

Make sauce as follows and serve with rissoles:

Mix balance of tomato juice, balance of lemon juice and milk together with tomato puree.

Heat another frying pan with 1 tablespoon oil. Pour above into same and bring to boil.

Now add cornflour, which has been dissolved in $\frac{1}{4}$ cup cold water. Stir well. If not thick enough, add more cornflour. Serve with mashed potatoes.

* MEXICAN FISH

2 lb. Fish (Cod or any other
    firm fish)
2 Onions
1 Clove
1 Green Pepper (sliced in rings)
    Salt and Pepper
1 Bayleaf

2 Tablespoons Sunflower or
    Corn Oil
1 10 oz. tin Mushrooms
1 Wineglass White Wine
2 Large Tomatoes (skinned
    and sliced)

Method: Slice fish and steam in a little water together with one onion, bayleaf and clove, until soft.

Slice the other onion and fry in hot oil until golden brown. Gently add green peppers and tomatoes and simmer for 10-15 minutes. Then add mushrooms, wine, pieces of steamed fish, salt and pepper, to taste.

Cook for a further 15 minutes.

* FILLETED FISH

1 lb. any filleted line fish
1 lb. Filleted Cod
1 Egg White
1 Thick slice of Bread (with-
    out crusts)
    Little Parsley (optional)
    Little Water

Fish bones and skin, if possible
1 Onion
1 Teaspoon Vinegar
2 or 3 Medium Carrots
1 Teaspoon Cinnamon
    Salt and Pepper

Method: Mince fish, onion, bread and parsley. Add egg white, vinegar, cinnamon, salt and pepper and mix well. Add sufficient cold water to make a soft but firm paste.

While preparing fish, fill a large saucepan half full with water, fish bones, fish heads and skins, if any, salt to taste, sliced carrots and onion and bring to boil.

Roll minced fish mixture into balls, with wet hands, and gently add the balls to the boiling water.

Cover and gently cook for $1\frac{1}{2}$-2 hours. Remove carefully from saucepan when cold, place a slice of the boiled carrot on each ball and strain the gravy over the top. Serve hot or cold. Can be kept in refrigerator for a few days.

✴ SALMON MOULD

1 Tin Pink Salmon
1 8 oz. tin grilling or Button
   Mushrooms
  Salt and Pepper

2 Teaspoons Gelatine
1 Onion (finely chopped)
Tomato

Method: Put mushrooms and juice into small saucepan, add salt and pepper to taste and bring to boil.

Dissolve gelatine in $\frac{1}{4}$ cup boiling water and add to mushrooms and let same boil for a further 3 to 4 minutes.

Remove from stove and leave to cool. Mix salmon with chopped onion and place in a wet mould.

Pour cooled mushroom mixture over salmon and mix well.

Place in refrigerator to set. Remove from mould, decorate with thin sliced onion and tomato. Serve with boiled potatoes.

✴ BAKED FISH

Left over Fried Fish
$\frac{1}{4}$ lb. Skim Milk Cheese
  Juice of 1 Lemon
  Sunflower or Corn Oil

1 Tomato, sliced
Salt and Pepper
Sliced par-boiled Potatoes

Method: Line ovenware dish with tomato, cover with cut up fried fish. Season with salt and pepper and add lemon juice.

Cover with sliced potatoes and sprinkle with oil.

Put in oven (400°) and bake until potatoes are brown and soft.

✴ CHOPPED HERRING

3 Salt Herrings
1 Small peeled Apple
4 Water Biscuits
$\frac{1}{4}$ Cup Vinegar

White of 1 hard-boiled Egg
1 Small Onion
Pinch Cinnamon
1 Teaspoon Sugar

Method: Clean and soak herrings in water overnight or for about 9 to 10 hours. Remove skin and bones.

Mince herrings, apple, onion and biscuits. Mix with vinegar, sugar and cinnamon. Arrange on platter.

Remove the yolk from egg, chop up white and decorate the herrings. Sliced tomato can also be added for decoration.

* PILCHARDS IN TOMATO SAUCE

Empty tin of pilchards and its sauce into saucepan with salt, pepper and Worcester sauce to taste. Heat and serve on toast, or with mashed potatoes.

* FISH AND POTATO FRY

Left over Boiled or Baked Potatoes	Salt and Pepper
Onions	Lemon Juice
Left over Fried Fish	Sunflower or Corn Oil

Method: Chop onions fine and fry in hot oil with diced potatoes. Add cut-up fish, salt, pepper and lemon juice and fry until golden brown.

You will notice that veal is used a good deal in the recipes and this is because veal is the leanest of meats and is therefore specially recommended. Beef and chicken are also allowed, provided the fat is removed before cooking, but mutton and lamb are not recommended due to the difficulty in removing the fat (and really lean mutton or lamb is not easily procurable).

To bring out the full flavour of veal, I use lemon juice and ginger quite lavishly. Where these ingredients are not given in the recipes, they can still be used, if desired.

All meat and chicken should be well washed and dried and all fat must be removed before cooking.

You will notice that in most recipes for chicken, the chicken is first boiled for a short while. This has the effect of removing any surplus fat.

✳ ROAST LEG OF VEAL

Leg of Veal   Lemon Juice
Salt, Pepper, Ginger   Sunflower or Corn Oil
1 Onion (optional)

Method: Squeeze lemon juice over meat, season well with salt, pepper and ginger.

Put a little oil in roasting pan and put in leg of veal with the onion.

Cover, and cook in oven at 450° until brown and tender.

Allow 30-35 minutes per lb.

✳ ROAST SHOULDER OF VEAL

2½ lb. Shoulder of Veal   Salt and Pepper
Ground Ginger   Lemon Juice
1 Onion

Method: Squeeze lemon juice over meat, season with salt and pepper and sprinkle with a good helping of ginger. Parcel meat, with the onion, loosely in thick tinfoil and roast in hot oven (450°) for 1¾ hours. Open up tinfoil and allow meat to get slightly brown.

✳ ROAST LOIN OF VEAL

2½-3 lb. Loin of Veal   Lemon Juice
  Salt and Pepper   Ground Ginger
  Onion   Water
  Flour

Method: Squeeze juice of lemon over meat, salt and pepper same. Leave for 10-15 minutes.

Sprinkle well with ground ginger and rub same in with the back of a spoon.

Put in roasting pan with ½-1 cup of water and onion, cut in four. Cover pan and put into oven (450°), basting at intervals until meat is tender. More water can be added, if necessary.

When meat is tender, uncover and leave to brown. To make gravy, remove some of the liquid from pan and put into small saucepan. Mix 2 teaspoons flour with ¼ cup water until creamy. Gradually add this to the hot liquid and stir over medium heat until thickened. More flour and water can be added if not thick enough.

✳ POT ROAST BREAST OF VEAL

2½ lb. Breast of Veal   Juice of 1 Lemon
3 Tablespoons Sunflower or Corn Oil   3 Cups warm Water
1 Onion   Salt and Pepper
2 Bayleaves (optional)   Ginger
6 Peppercorns (optional)   2 Teaspoons Cornflour

Method: Squeeze lemon juice over meat and let stand for about 10-15 minutes. Add salt and pepper and rub in good helping of ginger. Heat oil in large saucepan, add meat and sliced onion and brown.

Add water, bayleaves and peppercorns, cover saucepan with lid, turn heat down and let simmer for 60 minutes, or until meat is tender. More water may be added, if necessary. Dissolve 2 teaspoons cornflour with $\frac{1}{4}$ cup cold water, add to gravy to thicken.

✱ STUFFED RAISED SHOULDER OF VEAL

2-3 lb. Raised Shoulder of Veal	Lemon Juice
Salt and Pepper	Ginger

Method: Wash meat, squeeze on lemon juice, leave to stand for 10-15 minutes.

Season with salt and pepper and sprinkle generously with ginger.

Stuffing:

$\frac{1}{2}$ lb. Beefsteak	1 small Onion
1 Inch slice of Bread, without crust	Pinch Mixed Herbs
1 Tablespoon Parsley	Salt and Pepper
A little cold Water to mix	

Method: Mince meat, onion and bread together. Add herbs, parsley, pepper and salt, moisten mixture with water.

Insert mixture in veal, roll and secure with skewers or sew up with cotton.

Put rolled veal into roasting pan containing oil about $\frac{1}{4}$ inch deep. Cover pan and roast in oven (450°) allowing 30-35 minutes per lb., or until meat is tender and browned.

✱ VIENNA SCHNITZEL

4 Thin slices boneless Veal	Breadcrumbs
1 Egg White	Salt and Pepper
Sunflower or Corn Oil	Lemon Juice

Method: Squeeze lemon juice over meat, salt and pepper same and leave for 15 minutes. Dip meat into breadcrumbs, then into slightly beaten egg white and again into the breadcrumbs. Put into refrigerator for about one hour. Fry, in medium hot oil, slowly. Oil must not cover the meat.

Serve with a slice of lemon and anchovy or capers on top of schnitzel.

✱ VEAL STEW

2 lb. Veal
2½ Tablespoons Sunflower or
    Corn Oil
  Ginger
½ Cup Parsley
½ Cup White Wine (optional)
1 Lemon

Salt and Pepper
2 Large Tomatoes
1 Onion
2 Bayleaves ⎫
6 Peppercorns ⎬ optional
  Pinch of Thyme ⎭

Method: Squeeze lemon juice over meat and cut into pieces.
Sprinkle with salt, pepper, ground ginger and pinch of thyme.
Brown meat and sliced onion in the hot oil. In the meantime par-
boil potatoes in half a pot of water to which salt has been added.

When meat is brown, add bayleaves, peppercorns, parsley and
about a cup of the potato water and the skinned and sliced
tomatoes and wine.

Turn heat down and let same simmer until meat is tender.

When the potatoes are par-boiled, remove from water and add
to meat mixture about an hour before serving. Other vegetables
can also be added to the stew, if desired. Instead of the potato
water, the juice of a tin of mushrooms can be used. The mushrooms can also then be added to the meat about 10 minutes
before serving. In this case, the potatoes should be properly
boiled and served separately.

✱ VEAL AND MUSHROOMS

6 Slices of Veal Steak
1 Large Onion, sliced
  Salt and Pepper
  Pinch of Thyme and Mixed
    Herbs
1 Cup White Wine
1 10 oz. tin Button Mushrooms

3 Tablespoons Sunflower or
    Corn Oil
  Juice of 1 Lemon
2 Bayleaves
  Parsley
2 Large Tomatoes, peeled
  and sliced

Method: Wash veal well, squeeze lemon juice over same and
leave for 15-20 minutes. Add salt and pepper.

Heat oil in pan and brown veal and onions.

Lower heat and add thyme, mixed herbs, bayleaves, parsley,
wine, tomatoes and juice of the tin of mushrooms. Cover pan

and simmer until tender, about 1 hour. 10 minutes before serving,
add the mushrooms.

✳ JELLIED VEAL LOAF

1½ lb. Shoulder of Veal   1 Onion
1 Knuckle of Veal (sawn into pieces)   2 Tablespoons Vinegar
2 Teaspoons Salt   2 Large cooked Beetroot

Method: Cover meat and bone with boiling water. Add onion
and vinegar and cook until tender.

Remove meat, and leave liquid in uncovered pot to simmer
until there is only 1½ cups left. Cut up meat into small pieces.

In bottom of wet mould, arrange slices of beetroot, cover with
layer of meat and continue until meat and beetroot are finished.
Pour liquid over slowly and chill until set. (A little granulated
gelatine can be added to the liquid if it does not set stiff enough.)

✳ VEAL MARENGO

2 lb. Stewing Veal   2 Cups Water
  Flour   Salt and Pepper
½ Cup dry White Wine   2 Onions, sliced
4 Tablespoons Tomato Puree   1 Clove Garlic, thinly sliced
  Pinch Mixed Herbs   1 Teaspoon Sugar
  Pinch of Thyme   6 Peppercorns
  Parsley   2 Bayleaves
1 10 oz. tin Button Mushrooms   2 Teaspoons Lemon Juice
  or ½ lb. fresh Mushrooms,   1 Teaspoon Ginger
  thinly sliced   Croutons of Fried Bread
  Sunflower or Corn Oil
  (2-3 Tablespoons)

Method: Wash and dry the meat and cut into 1½ inch cubes. Well
season some flour with salt and pepper (paprika may be used if
liked) and toss the meat into it. Heat oil in a pan and cook the
veal in it rather quickly, turning frequently until brown. Add the
onions and garlic, lower heat and cook until tender. Stir in 1
tablespoon flour and cook for a further 1-2 minutes. Stir in the

wine and water and, if using tinned mushrooms, the juice of same in which case use a little less water, and bring to the boil.

Add the tomato puree, herbs, sugar, lemon juice and ginger and season to taste with salt and pepper.

Cover the pan and simmer gently for 1 hour. Add the prepared mushrooms and cook for 10 minutes, or until they are tender. Serve with croutons.

Croutons: Cut two slices of bread into about $\frac{1}{2}$ inch squares and fry in very little hot oil until golden brown.

* VEAL IN CASSEROLE

6 Thin slices Veal Steak	Lemon Juice
Breadcrumbs	$\frac{1}{2}$ Cup Water
1 Tablespoon Sunflower or	Salt and Pepper
Corn Oil	1 Large Onion, sliced
1 Large Tomato, peeled and sliced	$\frac{3}{4}$ lb. Potatoes

Method: Wash and dry meat and squeeze lemon juice over and leave for 20 minutes.

Season with salt and pepper and dip into breadcrumbs.

Oil a casserole dish, line with a layer of onion and a layer of tomato. Add crumbed meat.

Slice potatoes into about $\frac{1}{4}$ inch-thick rounds and cover meat with same.

Pour water into dish and sprinkle top of potatoes with oil. Cover dish and put into oven (450°) for 1 hour or until meat and potatoes are soft.

* BRAISED VEAL CHOPS

6 Veal Chops	Salt and Pepper
Lemon Juice	1 Onion, sliced
Ginger	8 Allspice or Peppercorns
2 Bayleaves	2 Teaspoons Cornflour
2 Cups hot Water	
3 Tablespoons Sunflower or Corn Oil	

Method: Squeeze lemon juice over meat, add salt and pepper and a good helping of ginger.

Heat oil in saucepan and slightly brown meat and onions.
Add hot water, bayleaves and allspice or peppercorns.

Boil for 10 minutes then turn down heat, cover saucepan and
let same simmer for about 1 hour or until meat is tender. (Add
more water if needed.) Thicken gravy with 2 teaspoons cornflour which has been dissolved in ¼ cup of cold water.

If desired, par-boil potatoes and add same to the meat in
saucepan about 30 minutes before serving and let same simmer
with the meat. If gravy still needs thickening add cornflour as
mentioned above.

✱ VEAL IN WINE AND ORANGE SAUCE

3½ lb. Shoulder of Veal	Juice of 1 Lemon
Ginger	Salt and Pepper
Sunflower or Corn Oil	1 Onion, sliced
Cold Water	2 Bayleaves, 6 Allspice
Peeled Potatoes	½ Cup Semi-sweet White Wine
½ Cup Orange Juice	1 8 oz. tin Button Mushrooms
1 Tablespoon Cornflour	and juice

Method: Squeeze lemon juice over meat and leave for 15 minutes.
Rub in a good helping of ginger and add seasoning. Heat a little
oil in a large saucepan and brown meat. Add onions and brown.
Add water to cover meat and add allspice and bayleaves. Cover
saucepan, turn down heat and boil gently for 1 hour. (More water
may be added if necessary.)

Now add as many potatoes as required and let all simmer together until meat is almost tender. Remove meat and place in an
oiled roasting pan, leaving potatoes in the saucepan to get soft.
Make a sauce by mixing wine, orange juice, mushroom juice and
½ cup of the meat stock together. Add cornflour which has been
dissolved in a little mushroom juice. Pour over meat and place
in oven (350°) for 30 minutes. Add sliced mushrooms and leave
for a further 10 minutes. Serve with the potatoes left simmering.

✱ STUFFED VEAL WITH MUSHROOMS

3-3½ lb. Shoulder of Veal (boned by the butcher)	Lemon Juice
	Salt, Pepper, Ginger

Method: Wash meat, squeeze on lemon juice and leave to stand for 10 minutes. Season with salt and pepper and sprinkle generously with ginger.

Stuffing:

½ lb. Mushrooms (sliced)	1 Tablespoon Breadcrumbs
½ Green Pepper, chopped fine	2 Tablespoons Sunflower or
Salt and Pepper	Corn Oil
1 Onion, chopped fine	

Leave a few mushrooms for sauce.

Brown onions, green peppers and sliced mushrooms in hot oil. Add salt and pepper to taste. Fry for 5 minutes, then add breadcrumbs and fry for 1 minute more. Remove mushroom mixture from pan, leaving balance of oil in pan to fry balance of mushrooms for sauce.

Stuff veal with mushroom mixture and tie carefully with string. Place meat in casserole dish with about 4 tablespoons of oil and 1 onion cut in half.

Cover and cook in oven at 350° until meat is soft. A little water may be added if necessary. Cover may be removed a little while before serving to brown the meat.

Sauce: Make sauce before serving. Fry balance of mushrooms in left-over oil. Add some of the liquid from the meat and bring to boil. Thicken with cornflour.

Serve separately as a sauce.

✱ VEAL KNUCKLE STEW

2-3 Knuckles of Veal—cut up	2 Cloves Garlic (chopped fine)
3-4 Tablespoons Sunflower or	Flour
Corn Oil	Salt and Pepper
1 Large Onion (chopped fine)	2 Bayleaves
¾ Cup Semi-sweet Wine	Pinch Rosemary ⎫
1 Carrot (finely grated)	Pinch Sage ⎬ optional
¼ Cup Celery (chopped fine)	1 Small Tin Tomato Paste

Method: Ask your butcher to cut the veal knuckles into thickness of about 2 inch pieces. Wash and dry meat. Season some flour well with salt and pepper and toss the meat into it. Heat oil in a large saucepan and cook veal in it rather quickly, turning frequently until slightly brown—about 7-12 minutes.

Add onions and garlic and cook for further 2-3 minutes. Add bayleaves, wine, carrots, celery, rosemary and sage and tomato paste. Cook for further 5 minutes then cover with hot water or stock. Turn down heat and let simmer for 1½ hours, or until meat is tender.

Before serving, grate rind of lemon, put in frying pan with ½ cup wine and boil for 2 minutes before pouring into stew. Add more salt and pepper if required.

✳ BOILED SALTED TOPSIDE

3-4 lb. Lean Salted Topside	1 Carrot, sliced
1 Onion, sliced	6 Allspice or Peppercorns
2 Bayleaves	Water

Method: Remove any fat from meat, place in large saucepan with cold water to cover.

Add sliced carrot, onion, allspice or peppercorns and bayleaves, cover and bring to boil for about 10-15 minutes.

Turn down heat and let boil gently for 3 hours or until meat is tender. More water can be added if necessary.

✳ ROASTED STUFFED FILLET STEAK

2½-3 lb. Fillet, in one piece	1 Onion
Salt and Pepper	Water

Method: Make a pocket in the steak by cutting an incision down the centre, leaving the back and one inch on either side uncut.

Season meat with salt and pepper and fill with stuffing.

Close pocket by sewing or fasten with skewers.

Put into roasting pan, or ovenware dish, with quartered onion. Pour in water, about ¼ inch deep. Cover with lid, or tinfoil.

Roast in oven at 450° for about 1½-2 hours, or until meat is tender.

Stuffing:

1 Cup Breadcrumbs	1 Egg White
1 Teaspoon chopped Parsley	½ Teaspoon Nutmeg
Salt and Pepper	Pinch Mixed Herbs
2 Teaspoons Lemon Rind	

Mix all above ingredients together.

✱ GRILLED FILLET STEAK

To grill fillet, the best way, if a griller is not available, is to turn stove on to broil, cut meat into slices, season and brush a little oil on both sides. Put slices on grill pan and grill each side for 3-5 minutes, depending on whether rare, medium or well-done steak is required. Leave oven door slightly open.

Another method is to oil base of frying pan, bring to very high temperature and add seasoned sliced meat. Fry each side 3-5 minutes as required.

*

If rump steak is used instead of fillet, it should first be tenderised, either by beating, or by using a tenderising agent. It will take slightly longer to cook than fillet steak.

✱ BRAZILIAN STEAK

Fillet Steak	Sunflower or Corn Oil
Salt and Pepper	3 Teaspoons Horseradish Sauce
Worcester Sauce	Sliced Bananas
Mushroom Ketchup	

Method: Cut as many slices of fillet steak as needed. Brush oil on both sides and grill for 5 minutes each side.

Place in a fireproof dish and season with salt and pepper.

Spread about 3 teaspoons prepared horseradish over the meat and top with a thick layer of sliced bananas.

Mix the juice from the grill pan with 1 tablespoon of oil and two tablespoons Worcester sauce and two tablespoons mushroom ketchup.

Pour this over the meat and bake for 10-12 minutes in a hot oven (450°) until bananas are slightly browned.

Serve very hot, at once.

✳ CHATEAUBRIAND

2 lb. Fillet of Steak, in one piece
3 Tablespoons Sunflower or
   Corn Oil

$\frac{1}{4}$ Cup White Wine
1 Large Onion
Salt and Pepper

Method: Remove all fat from fillet, wash and dry. Season with pepper and salt and put into shallow Pyrex dish. Pre-heat stove for grilling. Heat oil in small frying pan and brown onions. When brown, put onions aside and pour hot oil over the fillet. Place fillet in stove and grill for about 10 minutes each side, basting in-between time. Add fried onions and wine.

Turn oven down to 300° and leave in oven for a further 15-20 minutes, continuing basting.

✳ BRANDY FILLET STEAK

Fillet Steak
2 Onions, sliced in thin rounds
$\frac{3}{4}$-1 Wine glass Brandy

Worcester Sauce
Salt and Pepper
$\frac{1}{4}$ Cup Sunflower or Corn Oil

Method: Cut the fillet into as many thin slices as required.

Season with salt and pepper.

Heat oil in frying pan and brown onions. Remove onions and put aside. Now place the slices of fillet in the hot oil and fry 3 minutes each side, then return onions to pan and add 1 teaspoon Worcester sauce for each slice of meat. Let boil for a minute or two, then add the brandy and set alight.

Serve with boiled potatoes and a cold salad.

Rump or sirloin steak can also be used but this takes slightly longer to fry.

* MONKEY GLAND STEAK

1 lb. Rump Steak	Salt and Pepper
2 Tablespoons Tomato Sauce	1 Dessertspoon Chutney
1 Dessertspoon Worcester Sauce	2 Teaspoons Cornflour
1 Cup cold Water	Sunflower or Corn Oil

Method: Cut steak into portions, wash and beat well to make soft. Add salt and pepper and fry in a little hot oil for about 5 minutes.

Add to above in frying pan, tomato sauce, Worcester sauce, chutney and mix well. Add cornflour which has been dissolved in the water and add to the above to make a thick sauce. Leave to simmer for a further 5-10 minutes.

* FRENCH STEAK

1 lb. Rump Steak	Salt and Pepper
2 Onions	

Method: Cut steak into suitable serving pieces and place in a casserole dish. Sprinkle with salt and pepper. Cut up onions and place on top of the steak.

Sauce:

2 Tablespoons Flour	$\frac{1}{4}$ Teaspoon dry Mustard
2 Teaspoons Worcester Sauce	$\frac{1}{2}$ Teaspoon Salt
2 Teaspoons Vinegar	2 Teaspoons Sugar

Mix these to a smooth paste with cold water, making it into a sauce of the white sauce consistency. Pour over the meat.

Cover casserole with lid, and simmer for three hours in a slow oven (250°).

6 Medium sized Fillet Steaks	1½ Cups dry Red Wine
1 Onion	2 Tablespoons Sunflower or
1 10 oz. tin Mushrooms and	Corn Oil
juice	1 Tablespoon Flour
6 Rounds of white Bread	

Method: Slice onions in fine rounds and brown in hot oil. Remove the onions and fry the bread until golden brown on both sides. Remove from pan and keep warm.

Slice mushrooms thinly and put into pan with the fried onions and wine and cook for about 5 minutes. Mix flour with juice of mushrooms to a creamy mixture, and add to mushroom and wine mixture to thicken. Season with pepper and salt and a little sugar if too sour.

Slightly season steaks, fry separately, 3 to 5 minutes each side, according to preference.

Place each steak on a round of fried bread and cover with the mushroom sauce.

✱ OVEN CRUMBED RUMP STEAK

4 or 5 Thinly sliced Steaks	1 Egg White
¼ Cup Wine	Breadcrumbs
1 10 oz. tin Button Mushrooms	1 Sliced Onion
Salt and Pepper	Pinch of Thyme (optional)
2 Large Tomatoes, skinned and	Pinch of Sugar
sliced	Sunflower or Corn Oil

Method: Season steaks with salt and pepper, dip into breadcrumbs, then into egg white and then into breadcrumbs again.

Fry in medium hot oil (oil must not cover meat).

When brown on each side and tender, remove meat from frying pan and place in Pyrex dish. In the same oil, brown sliced onion then add tomatoes, thyme, juice of the mushrooms and wine. Stir well until tomatoes are soft and smooth. Add mushrooms and let same boil for further five minutes. Throw this mixture over meat in Pyrex dish. Put into oven at 350° for about 15-20 minutes, basting at short intervals.

* BEEFSTEAK IN CRUMBS

1 lb. Steak
1 Onion
1 Tablespoon chopped Parsley
¼ Cup Water

1 Large Tomato
Salt and Pepper
1 Egg White
Breadcrumbs

Method: Mince meat and onion together. Add white of egg, parsley, water, salt and pepper. Mix well and form into balls.

Line Pyrex dish with sliced tomato, salt and pepper and a little water to cover.

Dip meat balls in breadcrumbs and place on top of tomatoes. Cover and bake at 400° for 30-40 minutes.

* MINCE BALLS IN CORNFLAKES

1 lb. Beefsteak
1 Onion
1 Inch thick slice of Bread
Pinch Mixed Herbs

1 Tomato, sliced
Salt and Pepper
½ Cup cold Water (approx)
Crushed Cornflakes

Method: Mince meat, bread and onion together. Add water to make a soft but firm consistency. Add salt and pepper and herbs. Roll into balls, flatten and dip into cornflakes. Line ovenware dish with slices of tomatoes and pour in sufficient water to cover bottom of dish. Add mince balls and bake in oven (400°) for 1 hour or until nicely browned on top. More hot water can be added if necessary.

* STEWED MINCE MEAT BALLS

1 lb. Beefsteak
1 Thick slice of Bread
1 Teaspoon Vinegar
2 Sliced Carrots
6 Peppercorns
Salt and Pepper

2 Onions
¼ Teaspoon Mixed Herbs
¼ Cup Water
3 Bayleaves
Potatoes
1 Teaspoon Cornflour

Method: Mince the meat with one onion and bread. Add salt, pepper and mixed herbs, vinegar and water. Mix all together and shape into balls.

Boil half saucepan of water with two sliced carrots, one whole onion, salt, bayleaves, peppercorns. When this comes to the boil, add mince balls, one at a time and let same boil for about 30 minutes, then turn heat to low, and let same simmer for about half an hour. Add as many potatoes as required and leave to simmer for a further two hours. Remove bayleaves and peppercorns and thicken gravy with cornflour mixed with $\frac{1}{4}$ cup of cold water.

✱ MINCE BALLS IN TOMATOES

1 lb. Beefsteak	1 Onion
1 Large slice of Bread	Good pinch Mixed Herbs
Salt and Pepper	Pinch of Saffron (optional)
1 Bayleaf	4 Allspice
3 or 4 Large Tomatoes	Cold Water
1 Teaspoon Sugar (optional)	Cornflour

Method: Mince meat, onion and bread together, season with salt, pepper and mixed herbs. Add sufficient water to make soft but firm mixture. Shape into balls.

Put into saucepan containing 3 or 4 cups boiling water, add bayleaf and allspice, cover and leave to boil for about 10-15 minutes, then turn down heat and let simmer for another 30 minutes or until there is very little water left.

Now add peeled and sliced tomatoes and saffron and leave to boil for further 15 minutes or until tomatoes are soft and pulpy.

Remove bayleaf and allspice and mash any remaining tomatoes which are pulpy until smooth.

Add sugar and thicken liquid with two teaspoons cornflour dissolved in $\frac{1}{4}$ cup of cold water. If not thick enough, more cornflour mixture can be added.

Boil for further minute or two, serve hot.

✱ SAVOURY MINCE ON TOAST

$\frac{1}{2}$ lb. Beefsteak	1 Pinch of Mixed Herbs
1 Tablespoon chopped Parsley	1 Tablespoon Sunflower or
2 Tablespoons Tomato Puree	Corn Oil
2 Teaspoons Worcester Sauce	Salt and Pepper
1 Small Onion	

Method: Mince meat and onion together. Add herbs, parsley, tomato puree, Worcester sauce, salt and pepper

Heat oil in small saucepan, add meat mixture, cover and cook on medium heat for about 30 minutes, stirring occasionally to prevent burning. Serve on toast.

✳ STUFFED TOMATOES

5 Large Tomatoes
½ lb. Beefsteak
1 Inch thick slice of Bread
1 Tablespoon Sunflower or
    Corn Oil

1 Onion
    Salt and Pepper
¼ Cup Water (approx.)
    Pinch Mixed Herbs (optional)

Method: Mince meat, onion and bread together. Add water to make meat mixture soft but firm. Add salt, pepper and herbs.

Cut off tops of tomatoes, scoop out pulp, some of which add to meat.

Fry meat mixture in hot oil until cooked (about 5 minutes).

Fill tomatoes with mixture and put into oiled Pyrex dish with a little water. Bake at 400° for about 45 minutes, or until tomatoes are soft.

✳ BEEF OLIVES

1½ lb. Stewing Steak
2 Sliced Onions
2 Tomatoes

    Salt and Pepper
2 Cups hot Water
    Sunflower or Corn Oil

Stuffing:
1 Cup Breadcrumbs
1 Teaspoon chopped Parsley
    Salt and Pepper
    Pinch of Mixed Herbs (optional)

1 Egg White
½ Teaspoon Nutmeg
2 Teaspoons Lemon
    Rind

Mix all together.

Method: Cut steak into thin slices about 4 inches square and season with salt and pepper. Spread with the stuffing, roll and tie with string both sides or fasten with toothpicks.

Brown sliced onions, then the olives in a little hot oil, being careful not to burn them.

When browned, add sliced tomatoes and two cups hot water.

Simmer for an hour, or until meat is tender. (More water can be added if necessary.) Thicken with flour.

✱ BEEF STROGANOFF

1 lb. Stewing Steak, thinly cut
1 Large Onion, finely chopped
1 Teaspoon Lemon Juice
1 Tablespoon red cooking Wine
2 Tomatoes, skinned and sliced
3 or 4 Mushrooms (optional)
1 Teaspoon chopped Parsley

2 Teaspoons Flour
$\frac{1}{2}$ Cup hot Water
Salt and Pepper to taste
Sunflower or Corn Oil
$\frac{1}{2}$ Teaspoon Sugar
1 Clove Garlic (optional)

Method: Cut steak into strips about $1\frac{1}{2}$ inches long and $\frac{1}{8}$ inch thick.

Brown quickly in a little oil. Add the chopped onion, garlic and tomatoes. Cook until tender.

Now add the lemon juice and stir. Sprinkle the flour over and blend well. Add the wine and continue to stir. Gradually add the hot water and stir until a gravy is formed.

Now add the salt, pepper, sugar and the sliced mushrooms and cook a little longer.

Transfer to a covered ovenproof dish and cook for about 15 minutes in a slow oven.

Before serving, stir in the chopped parsley.

✱ FORCED CABBAGE

1 lb. Beefsteak
Salt and Pepper
Bread—1 inch thick
Cornflour

2 Onions
Cabbage
Good pinch Mixed Herbs (optional)
Water

Method: Mince meat, onion and bread together, add salt and pepper and a little cold water to make soft but firm mixture.

Herbs may be mixed in, if desired.

Take leaves off the cabbage, wash well then pour boiling water over same and leave for a few minutes to soften. Remove from hot water carefully and fill each leaf with about a dessertspoon full, or more, of the minced meat. Roll leaf up, secure with toothpicks and put into a large saucepan with two cups water, the other onion and 1 teaspoon salt. Cover and boil for 10 minutes, then turn down heat and let same simmer until cabbage and meat are well cooked.

This must be watched as when the water boils away, more water must be added.

After about an hour, cabbage and meat should be cooked.

The gravy can then be thickened with about 1 tablespoon cornflour dissolved in $\frac{1}{4}$ cup cold water.

* SWEET AND SOUR FORCED CABBAGE

The method of preparation is the same as for forced cabbage, except when meat is done, add $\frac{1}{4}$ teaspoon tartaric acid and about 2 to 3 teaspoons sugar to the gravy, stir and leave for a further 15 minutes. If not sweet or sour enough, more sugar or tartaric acid may be added.

* SAUTE STEAK AND KIDNEY

4 Sheep's Kidneys	1 lb. Beefsteak
1 Onion	Salt and Pepper
2 Heaped teaspoons Cornflour	Water

Method: Remove fat and skin from kidneys, cut through centre and remove white core. Cut into pieces. Beat steak well to tenderise and cut into pieces. Put steak and kidney into saucepan, add salt, pepper and sliced onion, cover with water and boil slowly until meat is soft. More water can be added if necessary.

When meat is tender, allow water to boil away so that the meat will get brown. Now mix cornflour with $1\frac{1}{2}$ cups cold water and add to meat to make thick sauce. Boil for another minute.

*

This recipe can also be used for steak and kidney pie (See "Pastry B" for 2 crust pie) in which case roll out half of the pastry and line oiled deep ovenproof dish with it. Prick base. Add cooked meat mixture. Put an egg cup or pie funnel in centre to hold up pastry and cover with balance of pastry. Make a few slits in top pastry cover to allow steam to escape. Bake in hot oven (400°-450°) until brown.

✱ TOMATO BEEF STEW

1 lb. Beefsteak	2 or 3 Carrots
Salt and Pepper	4 Peppercorns
1 Onion	2 Bayleaves
Pinch of Thyme ⎫ optional	3 Large Tomatoes
¼ Cup Brown Sherry ⎭	3 Cups Water

Method: Wash and season meat, cut into small pieces and put into saucepan with finely chopped onion, 1 cup of cold water, peppercorns, bayleaves and pinch of thyme.
    Boil until water almost disappears.
    Add two cups of warm water, sliced carrots and skinned and sliced tomatoes and sherry. Turn down heat and allow to simmer until meat is tender.
    If desired, par-boiled potatoes can be added to above about ½ hour before serving.

✱ PICKLED WALNUT STEW WITH MEATBALLS

3-3½ lb. Boneless joint of Sirloin	5 Bayleaves
(or any other lean boneless Joint)	1 Onion, cut in half
4 Tablespoons Sunflower or Corn Oil	Salt and Pepper
10 Peppercorns	Ginger (optional)

Method: Wash meat well and remove any fat.
    Season meat with salt and pepper, sprinkle on a little ginger. In large saucepan, heat oil and slightly brown meat in same. Add onion and cook for further 3 minutes. Cover meat with hot water and add bayleaves and peppercorns. Cover pot and boil

for 1 hour, then turn heat down and simmer until meat is tender. More water may be added if necessary.

When meat is cooked, remove from saucepan and leave to get cold, also leave the stock to get cold, then remove any fat from top of same. This can be left in the refrigerator until the next day.

✳ MEATBALLS

1 lb. Beefsteak	1 Onion
1½ inch slice of Bread without crusts	1 Tablespoon chopped Parsley
6 Pickled Walnuts	Water
Salt and Pepper	Sugar
Flour	Vinegar (malt)

Method: Mince beefsteak with onion and slice of bread. Season with salt and pepper and add chopped parsley and sufficient water to make soft but firm mixture. Shape into small balls.

Bring meat stock to the boil in large saucepan (there should be at least 3 pints of stock). Add meat balls, cover and boil for about 20-30 minutes, until mince balls are cooked. (More water may be added if necessary.)

Cut up as many slices of the cold meat as required and add to the mince ball mixture and cook for about a further 5 minutes.

Meantime cut up pickled walnuts into small pieces with 1 tablespoon of the pickled walnut juice. Separately, mix 1 tablespoon flour with ¼-½ cup of malt vinegar, depending on amount of stock in saucepan, and add to cut-up walnuts. Add sugar to taste. Mix into meat mixture and boil for a further 5 minutes.

If gravy is too thin, more flour may be added to thicken.
Enough for about 10 people.

✳ SAUTE KIDNEYS

10 Sheep's Kidneys	1 Onion
Salt and Pepper	Water
½ Cup Flour	
2 Tablespoons Sunflower or Corn Oil	

Method: Pour boiling water over kidneys and remove skins and fat. Cut through the centre, removing the core, which is fatty.

Wash well, dry and cut each half into three pieces.

Heat oil. Season kidneys with salt and pepper, dip in flour and put into hot oil with sliced onions to brown. (Turn down heat and allow to brown slowly.) Add 2-2½ cups warm water—more if necessary.

Cover pot and let simmer until kidneys are tender.

Serve with mashed potatoes or rice.

✳ FRIED LIVER

1 lb. Calf's Liver   Salt and Pepper
Sunflower or Corn Oil

Method: Pour boiling water over liver and allow to stand for a few minutes, then remove skin. Slice, season with salt and pepper and fry in hot oil until brown and tender.

✳ CHOPPED LIVER

1 lb. Calf's Liver   1 Large Onion, sliced
½ Cup of Sunflower or Corn Oil

Method: Boil liver in salt water for 15-20 minutes until all blood has disappeared.

Fry onion in oil until golden brown.

Mince liver with fried onion, mix with as much of the fried oil as necessary to give a soft consistency.

Season with salt and pepper to taste. Decorate with hard boiled white of egg and sliced tomato.

✳ MEAT PANCAKES

2 Egg Whites   2 Cups Water
1½ Cups Flour (approx.)   Salt and Pepper
Sunflower or Corn Oil for frying

Method: Beat egg slightly, add water and mix. Mix in flour, salt and pepper. The mixture must be of a very thin consistency and put through a strainer so that there are no lumps. Heat small frying pan thoroughly, oil bottom of pan and pour in sufficient mixture to thinly cover same and fry on one side until firm. Throw unfried side of pancake on to dry cloth. Repeat until all the pancakes are made, piling one on top of the other. Fill fried side of pancake with cooked mince meat and fold over into envelope shape and re-fry in deep hot oil.

Filling:
Left-over cold Meat   Slice of Bread
Stock or Water

Mince left-over meat with bread, add a little stock or water to bind.

✱ COTTAGE PIE

Cold cooked Meat   1 Onion
Slice of Bread   Salt and Pepper
Mixed Herbs (optional)   Water
Sunflower or Corn Oil   Mashed Potatoes

Method: Mince cold cooked meat with onion and slice of bread. Add sufficient water to make soft mixture, pepper and salt to taste and add mixed herbs. Oil ovenproof dish, put in meat mixture, cover with mashed potato and bake in oven at 400° for 30 minutes, or until golden brown.

✱ BAKED MINCE LOAF

1 lb. Beefsteak   1 Tablespoon chopped
1 Large slice of Bread (about   Parsley
    1 inch thick without crusts)   Pinch of Mixed Herbs and
1 White of Egg   Thyme
  Salt and Pepper $\frac{3}{4}$-1 Cup cold Water
1 Onion

Method: Mince steak, onion and bread together. Mix in egg, spices and parsley. Add water gradually. The mixture must not be too stiff. Mix well. Add salt and pepper to taste.

Shape into loaf, place in oiled ovenware dish and bake in oven at 400° for about 35-45 minutes, or until nicely browned on top.

✳ BOILED CHICKEN

1 Boiling Fowl	Salt and Pepper
1 Onion (optional)	4 Peppercorns ⎱
Water	2 Bayleaves ⎰ optional

Method: Wash and clean chicken well, removing as much fat as possible. Season well with salt and pepper and boil together with the giblets in a little water until tender. An onion, 4 peppercorns and 2 bayleaves may be added if desired.

✳ ROAST CHICKEN

Roast chicken can be made in the same way as boiled chicken only when chicken is nearly tender, remove from stock, place into roasting pan and pour some of the stock (having first skimmed off all fat) over same. Add an onion, cover, and roast in oven at 400-450° for about 1 hour, or until brown and tender, basting continuously.

✳ SOUTHERN FRIED CHICKEN

2½-3 lb. Chicken	Sunflower or Corn Oil
Salt and Pepper	Breadcrumbs
Egg White	

Method: Clean and prepare chicken, season well with salt and pepper and boil as you would for boiled chicken. (See Boiled Chicken.)

Remove chicken when tender. Cut into portions.

Dip into slightly beaten egg white and then into breadcrumbs which have been seasoned with salt and pepper. Fry in hot oil, sufficient to cover chicken half-way, until golden brown.

✳ ROAST CHICKEN

Chicken   Salt and Pepper
Ginger (optional)   1 Onion, cut into quarters
Water

Method: Wash chicken well and remove as much fat as possible.
Season with salt and pepper and rub a little ginger into same.
Place chicken in roasting pan with the quartered onion and a little water. Cover and roast in oven at 450° until chicken is tender and brown, basting at intervals. (More water may be added if necessary.) Allow 20-25 minutes per lb.

✳ ROAST CHICKEN

Chicken   1 Onion
Salt and Pepper   Tinfoil

Method: Wash chicken well and remove as much fat as possible.
Season with salt and pepper. Parcel chicken and onion (cut in quarters) loosely in tinfoil. Roast in oven at 450° until chicken is tender and golden brown. Allow 20-25 minutes per lb.

✳ ROAST STUFFED CHICKEN IN GINGER ALE

2½-3 lb. Chicken   Salt and Pepper
3-3½ inch slice of Bread   1 Whole Onion
1 Small Onion, finely chopped   Pinch of Mixed Herbs
1 Tablespoon Parsley, finely   About 2 Tablespoons cold
    chopped   Water
1 Bottle Ginger Ale

Method: Clean and prepare chicken, removing as much fat as possible. Season with salt and pepper.

Stuffing: Cut off bread crusts and crumble the bread, add chopped parsley, chopped onion, herbs, salt, pepper and sufficient water to moisten mixture, which should still be crumbly. Stuff chicken with mixture and fasten with skewers.

Put chicken into roasting pan with the other onion, cut in half and pour ginger ale over same.

Cover and roast in oven at 450°, basting occasionally. Allow 25-30 minutes per lb., or until chicken is tender and golden brown.

✻ CHICKEN MORENGO

2-2½ lb. Chicken
1 Onion
Pinch of Thyme
2 Bayleaves
2 Small cups of White Wine
1 Large Tomato

2 Tablespoons Sunflower or Corn Oil
Salt and Pepper
1 Tablespoon Parsley
1 10 oz. tin Mushrooms

Method: Boil chicken for 10-15 minutes. Heat oil and brown sliced onion and chicken which has been cut up into portions. When brown, add salt, pepper, pinch of thyme, bayleaves and parsley and pour wine over same. Add peeled and sliced tomato and juice of mushrooms. Cover, and simmer until tender. About 20 minutes before ready to serve, add the mushrooms.

✻ HONG KONG CHICKEN

2½-3 lb. Chicken

Sauce:
2 Tablespoons Soya Sauce
1½ Teaspoons Monosodium
    Glutamate
2 Teaspoons Cornflour

1 Teaspoon Sugar
1 Teaspoon Salt
2 Tots Brandy
Sunflower or Corn Oil

Method: Flavour chicken well and steam for about 15 minutes, until fairly soft. Cut into portions.

Make sauce by mixing together Soya sauce, monosodium glutamate, sugar, salt. Add cornflour, which has been dissolved in half a cup of cold water, and two tots of brandy. Marinate chicken portions in above sauce for about 1 hour, remove chicken from sauce and deep fry same in hot oil, until golden brown.

Pour off oil and pour sauce over the chicken and let same simmer for 2-3 minutes. (If insufficient sauce, 1-2 cups warm water with more cornflour can be added.)

Serve with rice.

✴ LEFT-OVER ROAST CHICKEN

Cut chicken into portions. Put into Pyrex dish and pour over mushroom sauce (see Sauces).

Put into oven 450° for 20 minutes, basting continually.

Serve hot with rice or mashed potatoes.

If sauce is too thick, a little water or wine can be added.

✴ CHICKEN IN CORNFLAKES

Cut left-over chicken into portions, dip into slightly beaten egg white and then into crushed cornflakes.

Fry in medium hot oil until golden brown.

✴ PEKING CHICKEN

2-2½ lb. Chicken	2 Tablespoons Sunflower or
1 lb. Tin Pineapple chunks	Corn Oil
2 Tablespoons Worcester Sauce	Salt and Pepper
1 Cup White Wine	

Method: Wash and clean chicken well, removing as much fat as possible. Season with salt and pepper and boil for 10 minutes.

Remove chicken from saucepan, cut into small portions and brown in hot oil. When brown, add Worcester sauce, pineapple chunks with the juice and wine. Add salt and pepper to taste. Simmer until tender. If desired, sauce may be thickened with 2-3 teaspoons flour or cornflour five minutes before serving.

✱ CHICKEN IN ORANGE

2½-3 lb. Chicken
2 Carrots
2 Bayleaves
  Juice of 2-3 Oranges

1 Onion
  Salt and Pepper
4 Allspice

Method: Wash and clean chicken well, removing as much fat as possible. Season with salt and pepper and boil together with onion and grated carrots until tender but still firm.

Remove chicken from saucepan, and leave stock to get cold, then remove all fat.

Cut chicken into serving portions and place same in an oven-ware dish, together with bayleaves and allspice, add more seasoning if necessary.

Mix the orange juice with a little of the cold chicken stock to taste (must not be too sweet), and pour over the chicken.

Place in oven (400°) and leave until golden brown, basting frequently. Remove allspice and bayleaves.

✱ CHICKEN SUPREME

2½-3 lb. Chicken
  Salt and Pepper
  Ginger

1 Onion
3 Cups Water

Method: Season chicken with salt, pepper and ground ginger. Steam chicken in 3 cups of water with the onion, until tender. (More water may be added if necessary, keeping the water to no more than 3 cups.) Strain off the stock and put aside, removing all fat.

Cut up chicken into serving pieces and keep hot.

Sauce:
2 Tablespoons Sunflower or Corn Oil   2-3 Tablespoons Flour
1-2 Teaspoons Lemon Juice

Heat oil in small saucepan and gradually add flour, mixing well all the time to make a very thick paste. Add 1½ cups of the chicken stock to make a white sauce consistency. Mix well all the time.

Add 1-2 teaspoons lemon juice to taste. A little sugar may be added if required.

Serve separately at the table.

SAUCES

✳ WHITE SAUCE

1 Tablespoon Sunflower or Corn Oil
2 Tablespoons Cornflour (or Flour)
  Pinch of Pepper

1 Cup Skimmed Milk
½ Teaspoon Salt

Method: Mix cornflour (or flour) with ¼ cup of milk to a fine smooth paste then fill cup with balance of milk. Pour into saucepan, add oil, salt and pepper, and stir over low heat until it thickens and starts boiling.

Allow to boil for a minute or two, stirring continually so that the sauce is smooth. If sauce is too thick, a little more milk may be added. This sauce can also be made without the oil.

✳ SAUCE DE BERCY

2 small wine glasses of dry Red
  Wine
1 Tablespoon Sunflower or
  Corn Oil
1 Carrot, diced
¾ Cup Clear Soup Stock
2 Bayleaves
1 Large Tomato, skinned and
  sliced.

1 Small Onion, chopped fine
1 Medium sized Onion, sliced
1 Heaped Teaspoon Flour
1 Teaspoon Chopped Parsley
  Good pinch of Thyme
  Salt and Pepper

Method: Put the wine and one chopped onion in a small saucepan and boil wine down to 1 wine glass.

In another saucepan heat the oil and fry the carrots for 5 minutes, then add the sliced onion and fry until golden brown. Stir in flour, then add in stock, parsley, bayleaves, and thyme and simmer for 1 minute. Add tomato, salt and pepper and simmer for about 20 minutes.

Remove from heat and strain, and replace in saucepan. Strain wine mixture and add to above. Re-heat for 1-2 minutes and serve hot over grilled or fried steak.

✱ MUSHROOM KETCHUP SAUCE

1 Tablespoon Sunflower or
    Corn Oil
3 Tablespoons Mushroom
    Ketchup

2 Teaspoons Cornflour (or Flour)
2 Tablespoons Worcester Sauce
2 Tablespoons Tomato Sauce

Method: Heat oil and add Worcester sauce, mushroom ketchup and tomato sauce. When boiling, add cornflour dissolved in $\frac{1}{4}$ cup water to thicken.
    Boil for a further 2-3 minutes.

✱ TOMATO SAUCE

3 or 4 Large Tomatoes, skinned
    and sliced
1 Level Tablespoon
    Cornflour
    Salt, Pepper, Sugar
1 Tablespoon Sunflower or
    Corn Oil

$\frac{1}{4}$ Cup cold Water
    Good pinch each of
    Origanum, Coriander and
    Rosemary (optional)

Method: Boil oil and tomatoes together in small saucepan until tomatoes are soft and pulpy. Mash through strainer, making a puree. Discard pulp and pips and return puree to saucepan. Add herbs, bring to boil. Add cornflour, dissolved in $\frac{1}{4}$ cup cold water to thicken. Add salt, pepper, and sugar to taste. More cornflour may be added if not thick enough. Delicious served over boiled haddock or any other boiled fish.

✱ MUSHROOM SAUCE

1 10 oz. tin Button Mushrooms
1 Tablespoon Cornflour
    Salt and Pepper

1 Dessertspoon Sunflower or
    Corn Oil
$\frac{1}{4}$ Cup Wine

Method: Dissolve cornflour in $\frac{1}{4}$ cup mushroom juice, add to balance of mushroom juice. Mix in oil, wine and sliced mushrooms. Pour into small saucepan and boil for 5 minutes. Add salt and pepper to taste.

✱ ANCHOVY SAUCE

1 Cup Skimmed Milk	2 Teaspoons Cornflour (or Flour)
¼ Cup crushed Cornflakes	2 Teaspoons Anchovy Sauce
1 Tablespoon Tomato Puree	Pepper

Mix well and bring to the boil.

PUDDINGS

I find most steamed puddings made in the conventional way rather heavy and indigestible but made with oil, they are light and easily digested.

If serving custard with any pudding, use custard powder, as directed on the packet or tin, but substitute skimmed milk for any other milk mentioned. I am informed that there are no eggs in custard powder.

* BAKED ORANGE PUDDING

1 Tablespoon Sunflower or
    Corn Oil
1 Tablespoon grated Orange
    Rind
1½ Level Teaspoons Baking
    Powder

½ Cup Sugar
3 Tablespoons Flour (heaped)
2 Egg Whites
¾ Cup Orange Juice

Method: Mix oil and sugar. Add flour, baking powder, rind and orange juice. Mix well.

Fold in stiffly beaten egg whites. Bake in oiled casserole dish in oven 350° for 30 minutes.

* LEMON PUDDING

2 Tablespoons Sunflower or
    Corn Oil
2 Egg Whites
2¼ Level Tablespoons Flour

¾ Cup Sugar
1 Cup Skimmed Milk
    Juice of 1 small Lemon

Method: Mix oil and sugar well. Add flour, lemon juice and rind and mix well. Stir in milk and then fold in stiffly beaten egg whites. Pour into oiled ovenproof dish.

Place in pan of water and bake at 350° for 45 minutes or until top is golden brown.

✳ POACHED BANANAS

9 Ripe Bananas $2\frac{1}{2}$ Cups cold Water
1 Cup Sugar   1 Rounded Tablespoon Custard Powder

Method: Cut bananas in three and place in saucepan.
   Mix sugar and water together and pour over bananas.
   Bring slowly to boil. Cook gently for a further 5 minutes until bananas are soft and swollen but not broken.
   Mix custard powder with a little cold water to a smooth paste. Add same to banana mixture and simmer for a further 2 minutes.
   Serve hot or cold.

✳ CREOLE BANANAS

5 Bananas, sliced in rings
1 Tablespoon grated Orange
   Rind
Brown Sugar

3 Oranges, sliced in rings
3 Teaspoons Sunflower or
   Corn Oil
Rum, or Rum Essence

Method: Oil a shallow ovenproof dish.
   Place layer of oranges and layer of bananas in same.
   Sprinkle with sugar.
   Mix oil and orange rind together well, and dab it on top of fruit. Sprinkle with rum.
   Bake in moderate oven (350°) for 30 minutes.

✳ NUTTED PEACH

6-9 tinned Peach Halves
$\frac{1}{4}$ Teaspoon Mixed Spice
3 Tablespoons Brown Sugar
   Sunflower or Corn Oil

1 Tablespoon grated Orange
   Rind
2-3 Tablespoons Chopped
   Walnuts.

Method: Drain the peach halves and place in a shallow oiled ovenware dish.
   Mix together the mixed spice, grated orange rind, brown

sugar and chopped walnuts. Sprinkle mixture over peaches and bake in moderate oven (350°) for 15 minutes.

* APPLE TURNOVERS

3 Cups Flour	1 Teaspoon Salt
½ Cup Sunflower or Corn Oil	9-10 Tablespoons cold Water

Method: Sift together flour and salt, pour in oil and mix with fingers until particles look like breadcrumbs. Sprinkle cold water gradually over mixture until dough is moist enough to hold together. Roll out on lightly floured board to about ⅛ inch thick. Cut into ten 5 inch squares.

Filling:

⅔ Cup Sugar	1 Teaspoon Cinnamon
¼ Teaspoon Ground Cloves	(ground)
4 Cups Peeled and Sliced Apples	¼ Teaspoon Nutmeg (ground)
3-4 Teaspoons Sunflower or Corn Oil	

Mix together sugar, cinnamon, cloves and nutmeg. Divide the sliced apples equally among pastry squares. Sprinkle with sugar mixture and then with oil. Moisten edges of pastry and fold over to form a triangle, seal edges with fork and cut small slits in top to allow steam to escape.

Brush tops lightly with skimmed milk and sprinkle with sugar.

Bake in hot oven at 425° for 30-35 minutes and serve with orange sauce (see Pudding Sauces).

* APPLE AMBER

2 lb. Apples	2 Egg Whites
2 Tablespoons Sunflower or Corn Oil	3 Tablespoons Sugar (for egg white)
4 oz. Sugar	
Grated Rind and Juice of 1 Lemon	

Method: Peel and core apples and cook together with the 4 oz. sugar, oil, rind and juice of lemon. When soft, beat with a spoon until quite smooth. Pour into an oiled deep ovenware dish.

Whip egg whites very stiff and beat in remainder of the sugar (1 tablespoon at a time) until mixture stands up in stiff peaks. Pile this meringue on top of apple mixture and bake in 350° oven for 10 minutes, or until golden brown.

✱ APPLE CRISP

5 Cups peeled and sliced Apples	$\frac{1}{4}$ Cup Water
1 Tablespoon Lemon Juice	1 Cup Sugar
$\frac{1}{2}$ Cup Flour (sifted)	$\frac{1}{4}$ Cup Sunflower or Corn Oil
1 Teaspoon Ground Cinnamon	$\frac{1}{2}$ Teaspoon Ground Nutmeg

Method: Oil a Pyrex or ovenware dish, about 8 × 8 × 2 inches. (This oil is not included in the quantity given above.)

Arrange the sliced apples in bottom of dish. Mix water and lemon juice together and pour over apples.

Blend together sugar, flour, oil, cinnamon and nutmeg.

Sprinkle over apples.

Bake in moderate oven (375°) for 45 minutes.

✱ APPLE PIE

$\frac{3}{4}$ Cup Sugar	$\frac{1}{2}$ Teaspoon Ground Cinnamon
4-5 Cups Pared and Sliced Apples	1 Tablespoon Lemon Juice

Method: Make a two-crust pie pastry (See Pastry "C").

Oil and line an 8 inch or 9 inch pie dish with half the pastry.

Mix sugar and cinnamon together. Place apples alternately in pastry lined pie dish with sugar and cinnamon mixture.

Sprinkle lemon juice over apples.

Place top crust over filling. Seal and flute with thumb and fingers and cut slits in top of pastry to allow steam to escape.

Bake in hot oven (450°) for ten minutes and then at 350° for 40-50 minutes.

Sprinkle top with castor sugar.

* FRUIT BAKED APPLES

Wash and core as many large baking apples as required. Fill cavities firmly with a mixture of raisins, sultanas, sugar and pinch of ground cloves. Place apples in an oiled baking dish. Pour a little water over them and sprinkle a little sugar on each one.

Bake in oven at 350° for about 30 minutes, or until apples are tender. Place carefully on a serving dish and pour the syrup in the pan over them. Can be served hot or cold.

* PINEAPPLE AND PASSION FRUIT TART

1 Cup Sugar
1 Small Pineapple
4 Passion Fruit
1 Cup Water

2 Tablespoons Cornflour
1 Dessertspoon Sunflower or
   Corn Oil

Method: Bring sugar and water to boiling point. Add peeled and grated pineapple and juice of same. Simmer until pineapple is tender (about 15 minutes).

Blend cornflour with a little extra water until smooth.

Stir into pineapple mixture and simmer for 2 minutes.

Mix in oil and let simmer for further 2-3 minutes.

Remove from heat and add passion fruit pulp. Mix well.

Fill into baked shortcrust pastry (see page 91).

Serve with custard.

(Before filling pastry case, sprinkle the case with a mixture of flour and sugar to keep filling from soaking into pastry.)

* PEACH MERINGUE PIE

3 Egg Whites
  Pinch of Salt
$\frac{1}{2}$ Teaspoon Vanilla Essence

$\frac{1}{2}$ Teaspoon Cream of Tartar
$\frac{3}{4}$ Cup Sugar

Method: Beat egg whites very stiff. Gradually add cream of tartar and salt and continue beating. Add sugar, 2 tablespoonsful at a time, beating all the time, until meringue is dry and stiff enough to stand in peaks when beater is lifted. Beat in vanilla. Spread about ⅔ meringue on the bottom and sides of tinfoil lined 8 inch or 9 inch pieplate. Drop remaining meringue by teaspoonfuls around the side of the plate.

Bake in a slow oven (275°) for 30 minutes, then at 250° for a further 30 minutes, or until meringue is slightly brown and crisp. Cool on a wire rack.

Filling:

1 Cup Sliced Canned Peaches	½ Cup Peach Syrup
2 Teaspoons Lemon Juice	2 Heaped Teaspoons Cornflour
A little cold Water	

Bring peaches, syrup and lemon juice to boiling point.

Add cornflour, which has been dissolved in very little water.

Boil for 1-2 minutes to thicken. Cool and put into meringue case.

✱ STEAMED MINCEMEAT PUDDING

8 oz. Self-raising Flour	2 oz. Castor Sugar
3 Tablespoons Sunflower or	1 Heaped teaspoon grated
Corn Oil	Lemon Rind
1 Egg White	Little Skimmed Milk
Fruit Mincemeat	

Method: Sift flour into a bowl and add sugar. Mix in oil until same resembles fine breadcrumbs. Sprinkle in grated lemon rind.

Beat egg white well and add to flour mixture, mixing to a soft dry dough that can be handled, adding a little milk if it is too dry.

Divide into 3 portions of diminishing size, using smallest size to place at bottom of an oiled pudding basin, cover with mincemeat layer. (If desired, you can put a layer of mincemeat at bottom of pudding basin first.) Fill basin with layers of soft dough and mincemeat, finishing with layer of dough.

Cover with double piece of greaseproof paper and tie down securely with string and steam for about 1½-2 hours.

Turn out on to a serving dish. To decorate, add about a spoonful of mincemeat on top before serving.

Serve with Lemon Sauce or Brandy Sauce (see Pudding Sauces).

∗ STEAMED FRUIT PUDDING

8 oz. Self-raising Flour
3 Tablespoons Sunflower or
    Corn Oil
1 Tablespoon Skimmed Milk

2 oz. Castor Sugar
1 Egg White

    2 oz. Mixed Cake Fruit
    $\frac{1}{2}$ Teaspoon Cinnamon
    2 Teaspoons Sugar   } Mixed together
    1 Teaspoon grated Lemon Rind
    1 Teaspoon Brandy

Method: Sift flour and sugar into bowl. Mix in oil until same resembles fine breadcrumbs. Add mixed fruit. Add beaten egg whites to flour and fruit mixture. Lastly, add milk, mixing to a soft but dry dough that can be handled.

Make into ball and place into oiled pudding basin.

Cover with double piece of greaseproof paper and tie down securely. Steam for $1\frac{1}{2}$-2 hours. Turn out on serving dish and serve with sauce (see Pudding Sauces).

∗ RASPBERRY JAM STEAMED PUDDING

1 Cup Flour
1 Slightly heaped Teaspoon
    Baking Powder
1 Egg White
$\frac{1}{4}$ Cup Skimmed Milk
2 Tablespoons Sunflower or
    Corn Oil

1 Tablespoon Sugar
2 Tablespoons Raspberry Jam
$\frac{1}{2}$ Teaspoon Lemon Essence
    (optional)

Method: Mix oil and sugar well. Add egg white and beat well. Add jam, essence and milk. Mix well.

Add sifted flour and baking powder. Mix well.

Place mixture into an oiled pudding basin and cover with double piece of greaseproof paper and tie down securely with string.

Place basin into large pot, $\frac{3}{4}$ full of boiling water, cover with lid and steam for $1\frac{1}{2}$ hours. Ease sides with knife, turn out on to a serving dish and serve with a sauce (see Pudding Sauces).

✱ PUMPKIN FRITTERS

$1\frac{1}{2}$ lb. Pumpkin	$\frac{1}{4}$ Teaspoon Salt
$\frac{1}{2}$ Cup Flour, sifted	1 Level Teaspoon Baking Powder
2 Level Teaspoons Sugar	Sunflower or Corn Oil for frying

Method: Cook pumpkin in a little water until soft. Strain water off and mash pumpkin until smooth. Add salt, flour, baking powder and sugar and mix well. (If mixture is too stiff, add 2-3 tablespoons cold water.) Mixture must come off the spoon easily.

Drop tablespoonfuls into hot oil and fry each side until golden brown.

Serve with sugar mixed with a little ground cinnamon, if desired.

✱ BANANA FRITTERS

1 Cup Flour	$\frac{1}{2}$ Cup Skimmed Milk
$\frac{1}{2}$ Cup Cold Water (approx.)	Pinch of Salt
1 Tablespoon Sugar	$\frac{1}{4}$ Teaspoon Ground Cinnamon
$\frac{1}{2}$ Teaspoon Baking Powder	3 or 4 Bananas
Sunflower or Corn Oil	

Method: Sift flour, salt, sugar, cinnamon, and baking powder together. Add milk and mix well to remove all lumps. Stir in water to make a soft consistency as for pancakes.

Cut bananas into thin rounds and add to above mixture.

Heat a little oil in a large frying pan and fry tablespoons of the mixture at medium heat, until each side is golden brown.

* PINEAPPLE FRITTERS

Make these in the same manner as Banana Fritters, using thinly sliced pineapples in place of the bananas.

* JAM PANCAKES

1 Cup Flour
 Pinch of Salt
2 Tablespoons Water
 Jam
½ Teaspoon Ground Cinnamon

1 Egg White
¾ Cup Skimmed Milk
½ Teaspoon Baking Powder
1 Tablespoon Sugar

Method: Mix flour, salt and egg white together. Add milk and water and mix well so that there are no lumps. Lastly, add in baking powder.

Heat a small frying pan and moisten base with oil. Pour in thin layer of mixture and fry lightly one side and then the other side.

Remove from pan and spread jam on one side and fold over.

Repeat same with balance of pancakes until all the mixture is used up.

Mix cinnamon and sugar together and sprinkle over pancakes. Serve at once.

* COFFEE SPONGE CREAM

1 Cup Strong Black Coffee
2 Tablespoons Sugar
1 Teaspoon Vanilla Essence
¼ Cup Boiling Water

1 Cup Skimmed Milk
2 Egg Whites
2 Tablespoons Gelatine

Method: Mix coffee, sugar and milk in saucepan and bring to boil.

Remove from heat and allow to cool.

Add gelatine dissolved in boiling water and essence.

Leave until mixture half sets and then add the stiffly beaten egg whites. Beat all together and turn into wetted mould.

Serve with custard.

* BANANA CRÈME

1 Pkt. Red Jelly
4 Large Bananas
½ Cup Orange Juice

1½ Cups Boiling Water
1 Tablespoon Lemon Juice
2 Tablespoons Sugar

Method: Dissolve jelly in boiling water, add sugar. Stir in orange juice. Allow to cool until half set.

Mash bananas and pour lemon juice over same and continue to mash. Add banana mixture to cooled jelly mixture and whip all together well. Allow to set in mould or serving dish. A little sugar may be added if required.

* ORANGE PRESERVE

6 Oranges
  Juice of 1 small Lemon

Sugar
1 Teaspoon Ginger

Method: Peel oranges and weigh. Weigh equal amount of sugar.

Cut oranges into small pieces and put in saucepan with the sugar, lemon juice and ginger.

Boil for 10 minutes, stirring continually, then turn down heat and let simmer for about another 30 minutes, until syrup thickens. Can be used as dessert or jam.

* PINEAPPLE JELLY

1 Pineapple (finely grated)
2½ Cups Water
1 Pkt. Jelly (Cherry or Raspberry)

¾ Cup Sugar
2 Dessertspoons Cornflour

Method: Bring sugar, water and grated pineapple to boiling point.

Add cornflour, dissolved in ¼ cup cold water, and leave to boil for a further 5 minutes.

Remove from stove.

Mix contents of the packet of jelly with 1 cup hot water and add to pineapple mixture. Pour into mould and leave to set.

Decorate by covering with small balls scooped out of a sweet melon (or any other fruit) and about 5 or 6 halved glacé cherries.

* ORANGE DELIGHT

1½ Cups Orange Juice
2 Dessertspoons Gelatine
1 Egg White

1 Cup Sugar
½ Cup Boiling Water

Method: Dissolve gelatine in a little cold water, then add the boiling water. Mix well with the orange juice and sugar and allow to almost set.

Beat egg white very stiff, fold into the almost set orange mixture and then beat well.

Place in refrigerator to set.

* MARSHMALLOW PUDDING

20 Marshmallows
1 Dessertspoon Lemon Juice
Pinch of Salt

1 Cup Juice of Canned Pineapples
2 Egg Whites

Method: Place marshmallows and juice of pineapple in double boiler and steam until melted. Remove from stove and add 1 dessertspoon lemon juice. Mix and set aside until slightly jellied and pour into a glass bowl.

Beat egg whites with salt until stiff and fold into above mixture. Put into refrigerator and leave to set (about 4-5 hours).

Decorate with pieces of the canned pineapples and cherries.

* POTATO PUDDING

4 Large Potatoes, finely grated
1 Small Onion, sliced
½ Teaspoon Baking Powder
Salt and Pepper to taste
½ Cup Sunflower or Corn Oil

1 Tablespoon Flour
1 Egg White (beaten)
Oats

Method: Fry onion in hot oil until golden brown. Remove onions and let oil cool.

In a large bowl, mix together the grated potatoes, flour, baking powder, salt, pepper and egg white. Add the cooled oil, leaving a little to oil ovenware dish for baking.

Oil deep ovenware dish, sprinkle with oats. Pour in potato mixture and again sprinkle top with oats.

Bake at 350° for about 1 hour, or until golden brown. Can be served with any meat dish in place of ordinary potatoes.

PUDDING SAUCES

❋ LEMON SAUCE

½ Cup Sugar
1 Cup Water
1 Teaspoon grated Lemon Rind

1 Tablespoon Cornflour
2 Tablespoons Lemon Juice

Method: Blend together sugar, cornflour, grated lemon rind and water. Bring to boil and continue boiling and stirring for 5 minutes, until sauce thickens. Remove from heat and mix in lemon juice.

❋ WINE SAUCE

1 Tablespoon Sunflower or Corn Oil
½ Cup Skimmed Milk
  A few Drops Red Colouring

1 Tablespoon Flour
¼ Cup Port Wine

Method: Heat oil in saucepan, stir in flour and mix. Gradually add milk. Cook for 3 minutes or until mixture thickens. Add wine and red colouring. Sweeten to taste.

❋ BRANDY SAUCE

Bring 1 cup water, 1 cup sugar and the juice of ½ a lemon to the boil.

Dissolve 1 heaped tablespoon of cornflour in a little cold water and stir into sugar mixture, cooking until the mixture thickens. Lastly, add ¼ cup brandy and continue boiling for 1 minute. If the mixture is too thin, add extra cornflour.

❋ APRICOT JAM SAUCE

Add 1 cup Apricot jam to ½ cup boiling water. Stir over a low heat until jam melts. Dissolve 2 heaped teaspoons cornflour in a little cold water, add to jam mixture and cook until thick. A little brandy or wine may be added if desired.

✳ ORANGE SAUCE

3 Level tablespoons Flour
1 Cup Orange Juice
2 Tablespoons Sunflower or
    Corn Oil

$\frac{1}{2}$ Cup Sugar
$1\frac{1}{2}$ Tablespoons Lemon Juice

Method: Combine and mix thoroughly the above ingredients. Cook over low heat, stirring constantly until mixture begins to boil. Remove from heat.

I find baking with oil a real pleasure as it is so much easier to mix oil and sugar than to cream butter and sugar and, of course, measuring is simplified. The following hints may assist you:

Egg whites of extra large eggs are used in all recipes.

Before baking, always pre-heat oven to required heat so that oven is ready to put cake in as soon as the mixture is ready.

When baking pastry with a filling, always sprinkle a mixture of a little flour and sugar between pastry and filling, as this prevents the filling from soaking into the pastry. This also applies when putting hot filling into a baked pastry shell.

Fruit cakes made with oil improve if kept a few days. They can be kept for quite a long while if wrapped in greaseproof paper and placed in an airtight tin. Always wash and dry fruit well before using for fruit cakes.

To weigh jam or marmalade, slightly damp a piece of greaseproof paper and weigh jam on this .

To make sure a cake is properly baked, insert a warmed skewer into centre of cake and, if dry when withdrawn, cake is ready. Another way of testing is by touch: if it is firm to the touch, it is properly baked.

All cakes should be left in the baking tin for a few minutes before turning out onto a wire rack to cool.

* HOT WATER SPONGE CAKE

3 Large Egg Whites
1½ Cups Flour
3 Rounded Teaspoons Baking
   Powder
1 Teaspoon Orange Essence
½ Cup Water
1 Cup Sugar

Pinch of Salt
1 Dessertspoon Lemon Rind
4 Dessertspoons Sunflower or
   Corn Oil
Chopped Nuts
Apricot Jam

Method: Beat egg whites and salt very well. Add sugar gradually and continue beating for a further minute.

Meanwhile, mix water and oil together and bring to boil.

Sift flour and add to egg mixture, folding in lightly. Add lemon rind and orange essence. Mix well.

Now pour in half the boiling liquid then sprinkle in the baking powder. Add the balance of the liquid, mixing well in between additions.

Pour mixture into two 7-inch sandwich tins, which have been oiled and sprinkled with flour. Bake at 350° for 10-15 minutes, or until cake is baked. Leave in tins for about 3-5 minutes, then remove on to cake racks to cool.

When cold, sandwich together with jam. Spread jam on top of cake and sprinkle on chopped nuts.

✳ HOT MILK SPONGE SANDWICH CAKE

2 Egg Whites
1 Cup Flour
3 Teaspoons Baking Powder
2 Tablespoons Sunflower or
    Corn Oil

$\frac{3}{4}$ Cup Sugar
$\frac{1}{4}$ Teaspoon Salt
1 Teaspoon Orange Essence
$\frac{1}{2}$ Cup Skimmed Milk

Method: Beat egg whites very well, add sugar and continue beating until mixed well.

Sift flour, salt and baking powder together and add slowly to egg mixture. Mix in essence.

Meanwhile, have milk and oil (mixed together) just on the boil, and add same quickly to the other mixture. Pour into two 7-inch oiled sandwich tins and bake at 350° for 20-25 minutes. Sandwich together with apricot jam or other filling.

✳ ORANGE RING

4 Tablespoons Sunflower or
    Corn Oil
2 Egg Whites
    Grated rind of 1 Orange
    Pinch of Salt
8 oz. Icing Sugar

4 oz. Castor Sugar
2 Teaspoons Vinegar
4 oz. Self-raising Flour
2-3 Tablespoons Orange Juice
    A few Nuts (chopped)

73

Method: Mix oil and sugar well in a bowl. Add the egg whites, one at a time, beating well after each. Stir in the grated orange rind. Sift flour and salt together and fold into the mixture. Stir in 1 tablespoon of the orange juice and mix lightly. Pour mixture into a well oiled 7-inch tube tin.

Bake in centre of oven, at moderate heat (350°) for 30 minutes, or until firm to the touch.

Turn tin upside down on a wire rack. Leave cake in tin in this position to cool for about 30 minutes. The cake will gradually drop out of the tin onto the rack.

Icing:

Sift icing sugar into a bowl and mix in enough of the remaining orange juice to give a stiff coating consistency.

Spread icing over cake and decorate with chopped nuts.

✱ PINEAPPLE SANDWICH CAKE

2 Cups Flour
½ Teaspoon Salt
4 Tablespoons Sunflower or
    Corn Oil
½ Teaspoon grated Lemon Rind
¼ Teaspoon Vanilla Essence

4½ Level Teaspoons Baking
    Powder
1 Cup Sugar
¾ Cup Pineapple Juice
2 Egg Whites

Method: Sift together flour, baking powder, salt and sugar. Add oil, pineapple juice, grated lemon rind. Beat very well.

Add egg whites and vanilla essence and beat very well again.

Pour into two well greased and floured 8-inch sandwich tins and bake in moderate oven (350°) for 30-35 minutes.

Cool and sandwich together with pineapple filling (see Fillings).

✱ SIMPLE ORANGE CAKE

1 lb. Self-raising Flour
1 Level Teaspoon Baking Powder
6 Tablespoons Sunflower or
    Corn Oil

1 Cup Orange Juice
1 Cup Sugar
3 Egg Whites
    Rind of 1 Orange

Method: Mix sugar and oil well, add in egg whites one at a time, beating well after each. Add orange rind.

Sift flour and baking powder together and add to sugar mixture, alternately with the orange juice. Mix very well.

Oil an 8-inch cake tin and sprinkle base of tin with flour.

Pour mixture into same and bake at 350° for 1¼-1½ hours.

Can be eaten same day.

✱ ORANGE BLOSSOM CAKE

2 Cups Flour	½ Teaspoon Salt
4½ Level Teaspoons Baking Powder	1 Cup Sugar
4 Tablespoons Sunflower or Corn Oil	½ Cup Skimmed Milk
⅓ Cup Orange Juice	2 Egg Whites
1 Tablespoon grated Orange Rind	½ Teaspoon Vanilla Essence

Method: Sift together flour, baking powder, salt and sugar. Add orange rind, oil, milk and orange juice. Beat very well until batter is well blended. Add egg whites, unbeaten, and vanilla essence. Beat well.

Pour into two well oiled 8-inch layer pans (at least 1½ inches deep) and bake in moderate oven (350°) for 30-35 minutes. Fill with jam or any other filling.

Can be eaten same day.

✱ CONTINENTAL SPONGE CAKE

3 Egg Whites	6 oz. Castor Sugar
4 oz. Flour	1 Teaspoon Baking Powder
Apricot Jam	

Method: Beat eggs and sugar together in a bowl over a pan of hot water until mixture is thick and creamy. Remove bowl from heat and continue to beat for another 5 minutes.

Sift flour and baking powder and fold into mixture gently.

Pour mixture into 8-inch sandwich tin, which has been oiled and lined with greaseproof paper, and oil greaseproof paper.

Spread mixture evenly. Bake in moderate oven (350°) for 20-25 minutes, or until firm to the touch. Leave in tin for about 5 minutes then turn onto a wire rack to finish cooling.

Remove paper and cut cake horizontally to make sandwich. Spread one half with jam and place the other half on top.

Topping:

1 oz. Sultanas

1 oz. Glacé Cherries

6 oz. Icing Sugar

1 oz. Seedless Raisins

½ oz. Walnuts

A little warm Water

Method: Wash and dry sultanas and raisins. Cut each cherry in half. Chop walnuts into medium sized pieces. Sift icing sugar into a small bowl and add enough water to give a coating consistency. Beat well. Mix in fruit and nuts. Spread same over top of cake. Allow to stand in a cool place until icing sets.

✱ EGGLESS FRUIT CAKE

1 Cup Brown Sugar

1¼ Cups Water

1 Cup Seedless Raisins

2 oz. Mixed Peel

⅓ Cup Sunflower or Corn Oil

½ Teaspoon Salt

1 Teaspoon Ground Nutmeg

1 Teaspoon Ground Cinnamon

2 Cups Flour

5 Teaspoons Baking Powder

Method: Boil sugar, raisins, water, oil, nutmeg and cinnamon together. When on the boil, remove from stove and allow to cool.

Sift flour, salt and baking powder together and gradually add to sugar mixture. Finally, add the mixed peel, and mix very well.

Bake in a loaf tin (9 inches by 5 inches) oiled and greaseproof paper lined at 350° for ¾-1 hour.

✱ LIGHT FRUIT CAKE

8 Tablespoons Sunflower or
   Corn Oil
2 Heaped Teaspoons Baking Powder
8 oz. Castor Sugar
4 Egg Whites
1 Tablespoon Malt Vinegar
2 oz. Ground Almonds
2 oz. Blanched Split Almonds

11 oz. Flour
$\frac{1}{2}$ lb. Sultanas
$\frac{1}{4}$ lb. Raisins
$\frac{1}{4}$ lb. Currants
$\frac{1}{4}$ lb. Mixed cut Peel
2 Tablespoons Brandy
   Grated rind of 1 Lemon

Method: Mix oil and sugar well. Add lemon rind. Add egg whites one at a time, beating well after each addition. Add vinegar.

Sift flour and baking powder and add to mixture, alternately with the fruit. Add ground almonds and brandy and mix well.

Turn mixture into an oiled and lined 8-inch tin and decorate top of cake with blanched split almonds.

Bake at 350° for $2\frac{1}{4}$ hours.

✱ DARK FRUIT CAKE

1 lb. Mixed Cake Fruit
1 Cup Water
4 Tablespoons Sunflower or
   Corn Oil
2 Teaspoons Malt Vinegar
1 Heaped Teaspoon Baking
   Powder

$\frac{3}{4}$ Cup Sugar
2 Egg Whites
2 Cups Flour
1 Teaspoon Bicarbonate of Soda
1 Teaspoon Mixed Spice
2 Tablespoons Brandy
   (optional)

Method: Boil fruit, sugar and water for 5 minutes in large saucepan.

Take off stove and add oil. Leave to cool.

When cool, add unbeaten egg whites, one at a time, beating well after each with wooden spoon. Add vinegar.

Add flour, which has been sifted with bicarbonate of soda, and baking powder. Then add mixed spice and brandy. Mix well.

Turn mixture into an oiled and lined cake tin (8 inch). Bake at 350° for $1\frac{1}{4}$ hours.

¾ Cup Sugar
¾ Cup Flour
1 Teaspoon Baking Powder
¼ Teaspoon Salt

1 Teaspoon Vanilla Essence
½ Teaspoon Almond Essence
8 Egg Whites
1 Teaspoon Cream of Tartar

Method: Beat egg whites to a stiff froth, add cream of tartar and continue beating until egg whites are very stiff. Add sugar gradually, beating all the time. Sift flour, baking powder and salt. Fold lightly into first mixture. Add flavourings.

Put into an ungreased 9-inch tube pan. Bake at 350° for 50-60 minutes until cake shrinks slightly from pan. Remove from oven, invert on cake cooler. As cake cools it will loosen from the pan.

* RICH DARK FRUIT CAKE

¼ lb. Dates (stoned and cut
    in three)
½ Cup Boiling Water
12 Tablespoons Sunflower or
    Corn Oil
1 Tablespoon Malt Vinegar
3 Cups Flour
1½ Teaspoons Mixed Spice
1 Teaspoon Nescafé
½ lb. Currants
½ lb. Cherries (quartered)
2 oz. Glacé Pineapple (cut
    up)
1½ Cups Brown Sugar

1 Teaspoon Caramel
    Essence
1 Level Teaspoon Bicarbonate
    of Soda
2 Teaspoons Baking Powder
6 Egg Whites
¼ Teaspoon Salt
½ Teaspoon Nutmeg
½ lb. Raisins
½ lb. Sultanas
¼ lb. Mixed Cut Peel
2 oz. Ground Almonds
1 Teaspoon Vanilla Essence
1 Wine glass Brandy

Method: Soak dates in the bicarbonate of soda and boiling water. Leave to cool. Mix oil and sugar very well. Add egg whites one at a time, beating well after each. Beat in vinegar.

Add date mixture and mix well. Sift flour, baking powder, salt, spices and Nescafé together. Add to oil and sugar mixture, alternately with the fruits (which have already been mixed together). Add ground almonds, essences and brandy. Mix very well. Turn into a 10-inch or two 7-inch tins, oiled and lined with two thicknesses of greaseproof paper. Bake in oven (300°) for $3\frac{1}{4}$-4 hours.

* BOSTON BREAD

$2\frac{1}{2}$ Cups Flour
1 Cup Fruit (Dates, raisins,
    mixed peel, etc.)
1 Teaspoon Bicarbonate of Soda
    Pinch of Salt

1 Cup Golden Syrup
1 Teaspoon Ground Ginger
2 Teaspoons Mixed Spice
1 Cup Skimmed Milk

(Chopped nuts may be added with the fruit)

Method: Sift flour, mixed spice, ginger, salt and soda together.
    Melt syrup and mix with milk. Add liquid to dry ingredients and finally add the fruit.
    Oil 2 cocoa tins (1 lb. size) and half fill with mixture. Oil the lids of tins and cover. Stand tins in a large saucepan of boiling water (half full), cover saucepan and allow to boil for $2\frac{1}{4}$ hours on medium heat. Remove tins from saucepan, cool slightly and turn out.
    (Cocoa tins are only used if the proper tins are not to hand.)

* RAISIN CAKE

2 Cups Flour
$\frac{1}{2}$ Teaspoon Salt
$\frac{2}{3}$ Cup Raisins
$\frac{1}{2}$ Cup Sunflower or
    Corn Oil
3 Egg Whites
$\frac{2}{3}$ Cup Skimmed Milk

$4\frac{1}{2}$ Teaspoons Baking Powder
$\frac{1}{2}$ Teaspoon Ground Nutmeg
$\frac{1}{4}$ Cup Mixed Peel
1 Cup Sugar
1 Tablespoon Malt Vinegar
1 Teaspoon Vanilla Essence

Method: Sift flour, baking powder, salt and nutmeg together.
    Combine raisins and mixed peel with 2 tablespoons of dry sifted ingredients. Mix oil and sugar well, add egg whites one at a time, beating well after each, add vinegar.
    Mix together milk and vanilla essence and add alternately

79

with dry ingredients to oil mixture, beginning and ending with dry ingredients. Mix well after each addition.

Fold in floured raisins and peel. Pour into oiled and floured 9-inch tube tin. Bake in oven (350°) for 50-60 minutes.

✱ CHERRY CAKE

5 oz. Glacé Cherries
Pinch of Salt
6 oz. Castor Sugar
3 Egg Whites (lightly beaten)
12 oz. Self-raising Flour

6 Tablespoons Sunflower or
Corn Oil
Grated rind of 1 Lemon
¼ Cup Skimmed Milk

Method: Cut 4 oz. of the cherries into quarters. Sift flour and salt into bowl, add oil and mix until mixture resembles fine breadcrumbs.

Stir in the sugar, lemon rind and quartered cherries. Add the lightly beaten egg whites and mix well.

Stir in the milk to make stiff dropping consistency.

Put the mixture into an 8-inch oiled and greaseproof paper lined tin. Bake in moderate oven (350°) for 45 minutes or until firm to the touch.

Cool on a wire rack. Sprinkle with castor sugar and decorate with the remaining cherries.

✱ SPICY CURRANT CAKE

4 Tablespoons Sunflower or
Corn Oil
1 Egg White
8 oz. Self-raising Flour
1 Heaped Teaspoon
Mixed Spice
2 Teaspoons Lemon Rind

5 oz. Sugar
Pinch of Salt
1 Level Teaspoon Baking Powder
4 Tablespoons Skimmed Milk
12 oz. Currants (cleaned)
2 Tablespoons Lemon Juice

Topping:
1 Tablespoon Sunflower or
Corn Oil
2 Rounded Tablespoons
Brown Sugar

2 Rounded Tablespoons Flour
Good Pinch Ground Ginger
Good Pinch Ground Nutmeg
1 oz. Walnuts (chopped)

Method—Cake: Mix oil and sugar together well. Then add in egg white and beat well with a fork. Sift self-raising flour, baking powder, salt and mixed spice together and add to oil mixture, alternately with lemon juice and milk. Then fold in currants and grated lemon rind. Mix well together. Pour the mixture into a 7-inch cake tin, which has been oiled and lined with greaseproof paper. Smooth top of mixture to make it level.

Topping:

Rub oil into the plain flour and add the brown sugar, nutmeg and ginger. Mix well. Stir the walnuts into the mixture.

Scatter this over the mixture in tin and bake in centre of oven at 350° for 1¼ hours. (To test if cooked, insert a warmed skewer into centre of cake. If clean when withdrawn, cake is ready.) Leave in tin for 30 minutes then turn carefully out onto crumpled soft paper to protect topping. Then put, right side up, on a wire rack until cool.

✱ DATE AND WALNUT CAKE

1 lb. Dates (cut up)	6 Tablespoons Sunflower or
¼ lb. Shelled Walnuts (cut up)	Corn Oil
3 Egg Whites	1 Cup Sugar
4 Teaspoons Baking Powder	3 Cups Flour
2 Teaspoons Bicarbonate of	1 Teaspoon Mixed Spice
Soda	2 Cups Boiling Water

Method: Sprinkle bicarbonate of soda over dates and pour over boiling water and leave to cool.

Mix oil and sugar together, then beat egg whites one at a time into same. Add cooled date mixture and mix well. Sift together flour, baking powder and mixed spice. Add to above mixture alternately with the chopped walnuts. Mix well. Turn mixture into an oiled and lined 8-inch cake tin.

Bake in oven at 350° for 1¼ hours. (Test whether cooked by inserting warmed skewer into centre of cake. If clean when withdrawn, cake is ready.)

¾ Cup Sugar	1 Teaspoon Vanilla Essence
2 Tablespoons Sunflower or Corn Oil	1½ Cups Chopped Dates
	1 Teaspoon Bicarbonate of Soda
1 Cup Boiling Water	1 Teaspoon Cinnamon
2 Cups Flour	½ Teaspoon Mixed Spice
1 Teaspoon Ginger	2 oz. Chopped Walnuts

Method: Pour boiling water over sugar, oil, dates and bicarbonate of soda. Stir well and allow to cool.

Sift flour, cinnamon, ginger and mixed spice together and add alternatively with nuts to above mixture. Mix well.

Add vanilla essence.

Bake in oiled and floured medium size loaf tin for 45-55 minutes at 375°

✱ DATE CAKE

1 lb. Stoned Dates	2 Tablespoons Brandy (optional)
1 Cup Water	¾ Cup Sugar
4 Tablespoons Sunflower or Corn Oil	2 Egg Whites
	1 Teaspoon Malt Vinegar
2 Cups Flour	1 Teaspoon Baking Powder
1 Teaspoon Bicarbonate of Soda	1 Teaspoon Mixed Spice

Method: Cut up dates and boil in large saucepan together with sugar and water for 5 minutes. Take off stove and add oil. Leave to cool.

When cool, add unbeaten egg whites one at a time, beating well after each, with a wooden spoon, and add vinegar.

Then add flour which has been sifted with the bicarbonate of soda and baking powder. Lastly add mixed spice and brandy. Mix well.

Turn mixture into an 8-inch oiled and lined cake tin. Bake at 350° for 1¼-1½ hours.

* CHEESE CAKE

$\frac{1}{2}$ Cup Flour
1 Teaspoon Baking Powder
1 Egg White
1 Tablespoon Skimmed Milk
2 Tablespoons Sugar

1 Tablespoon Sunflower or
   Corn Oil
$\frac{1}{2}$ Teaspoon Vanilla Essence
   Pinch of Salt

Method: Beat sugar, oil and egg white together. Add flour, which has been sifted with baking powder and salt. Mix well. Add vanilla essence. Add milk gradually to mixture making it soft enough to spread with knife on pie plate. This is a thin mixture.
Oil pie dish and dust with flour.
Spread mixture thinly with knife all over pie dish evenly.
Pour in cheese filling and bake at 325° for 45 minutes.

Cheese Cake filling:
2 Egg Whites
1 Rounded Tablespoon Custard
   Powder
1 Cup Skimmed Milk

$\frac{1}{2}$ lb. White Skim Milk Cheese
4 Tablespoons Sugar
$\frac{1}{2}$ Teaspoon Vanilla Essence
2 Tablespoons Lemon Juice

Method: Combine cheese, custard powder and sugar. Add vanilla essence, lemon juice and milk. Mix well. Lastly, fold in well beaten egg whites and mix well. Bake at 325° for $\frac{1}{2}$-$\frac{3}{4}$ hour.

* MERINGUES

3 Egg Whites
1$\frac{1}{4}$ Cups Sugar

3 Teaspoons Baking Powder
$\frac{1}{4}$ Teaspoon Vanilla Essence

Method: Beat egg whites until stiff and dry. Gradually add two-thirds of sugar and continue beating until mixture holds shape and stands in peaks when beater is lifted. Fold in remaining sugar which has been mixed with baking powder. Add vanilla essence.
Line baking sheet with unglazed paper. Drop spoonfuls of meringue onto same and bake in slow oven (275°) for 45 minutes; turn off heat and leave in oven for a further 1 hour to dry out.

✱ PASSION FRUIT SANDWICH CAKE

4 Egg Whites	2 Cups Self-raising Flour
1 Cup Sugar	½ Teaspoon Baking Powder
½ Cup Sunflower or Corn Oil	Pinch of Salt
¼ Cup Passion Fruit pulp	1 Teaspoon Vanilla Essence

Method: Beat egg whites very stiff. Add sugar and salt and continue beating for a further 2 minutes.

Add passion fruit pulp, vanilla essence and oil. Lastly add sifted flour and baking powder. Mix very well. Pour into two oiled and floured 8-inch sandwich tins and bake in moderate oven (350°) for 20-25 minutes.

Allow to cool on wire rack and when cold sandwich together with the following filling:

2 Heaped Tablespoons Flour	Pulp of 2 Passion Fruit
½ Cup Orange Juice	1½ Tablespoons Sunflower or
1 Tablespoon Lemon Juice	Corn Oil
½ Cup Sugar	

Mix together thoroughly the above ingredients, cook over low heat, stirring constantly until mixture begins to boil and thickens.

✱ ORANGE LOAF

4 Tablespoons Sunflower or Corn Oil	⅓ Cup Skimmed Milk
1¼ Cups Sugar	2¼ Cups Flour
3 Egg Whites	3 Teaspoons Baking Powder
1 Teaspoon Vanilla Essence	¼ Teaspoon Salt
⅓ Cup Orange Juice	1 Tablespoon grated Orange Rind

Method: Mix oil and sugar together well. Add unbeaten egg whites one at a time, beating well after each.

Add vanilla essence, orange juice and rind. Sift together flour, baking powder and salt, and add alternately with the milk to first mixture. Mix very well. Bake in oiled and floured 10-inch by 6-inch by 3-inch loaf tin in moderate oven (350°) for 1 hour.

✱ BANANA AND WALNUT LOAF

4 Tablespoons Sunflower or
    Corn Oil
1 Cup Sugar
1 Cup ripe Bananas
2 Egg Whites

1¾ Cups Flour
1 Teaspoon Bicarbonate of Soda
½ Teaspoon Baking Powder
½ Cup chopped Walnuts

Method: Mix oil and sugar well. Sift flour, bicarbonate of soda and baking powder together.

Blend mashed bananas and flour alternately into oil mixture, mixing well after each addition.

Fold in stiffly beaten egg whites. Add nuts.

Bake in oiled and floured 10-inch by 6-inch by 3-inch loaf tin in moderate oven (350°) for 50-60 minutes.

✱ ORANGE SANDWICH CAKE

4 Egg Whites
1 Cup Sugar
½ Cup Sunflower or Corn Oil
½ Cup Orange Juice
1 Tablespoon grated Orange Rind

2 Cups Self-raising Flour
½ Teaspoon Baking Powder
   Pinch of Salt
1 Teaspoon Vanilla Essence

Method: Beat egg whites very stiff. Add sugar and salt and continue beating for a further 2 minutes.

Add orange rind, orange juice, vanilla essence and oil. Beat well. Lastly add sifted flour and baking powder. Mix very well.

Pour into two oiled and floured 8-inch sandwich tins and bake in moderate oven (350°) for 25-30 minutes.

Allow to cool on wire rack.

Sandwich together with orange filling (see Fillings) or with apricot jam.

✱ FRUIT AND MARMALADE LOAF

6 Tablespoons Sunflower or
    Corn Oil
2 Egg Whites
1 Level Teaspoon Baking
    Powder

4 oz. Sweet Orange Marmalade
6 oz. Sugar
8 oz. Self-raising Flour
4 oz. Mixed Cake Fruit

Method: Mix oil and sugar very well. Beat in egg whites one at a time.

Sift flour and baking powder together and fold half into oil mixture. Add fruit and marmalade folding them in lightly but well.

Fold in remaining flour.

Line a 9-inch by 5-inch by 3-inch loaf tin with greaseproof paper. Oil paper well. Put mixture into prepared tin and bake for $1\frac{1}{4}$-$1\frac{1}{2}$ hours in moderate oven (350°).

Cool in tin for about 10 minutes then turn onto a wire rack.

✱ SUNDAY CAKE

8 oz. Sugar

5 oz. Ground Almonds

1 Heaped teaspoon grated Lemon
    Rind

2 Rounded teaspoons Baking
    Powder

1 Tablespoon Lemon Juice

5 Tablespoons Sunflower or
    Corn Oil

4 oz. Flour, sifted

4 Egg Whites
    Pinch of Salt

1 Teaspoon Vanilla Essence

Method: Mix oil and sugar well together. Add almonds, lemon rind, lemon juice and Vanilla essence. Mix well.

Sift flour and baking powder and mix into above mixture.

Lastly, add very stiffly beaten egg whites, to which the salt has been added. Combine thoroughly.

Pour into an 8-inch baking tin which has been oiled and the base lined with greasproof paper. Bake in moderate oven (350°) for 40-45 minutes.

✱ DOUGHNUTS

2 Egg Whites

2 Tablespoons Sunflower or
    Corn Oil

$3\frac{1}{2}$ Cups Flour

$\frac{1}{2}$ Teaspoon Salt

$\frac{1}{4}$ Teaspoon Ground Cinnamon

1 Cup Sugar

$\frac{3}{4}$ Cup Skimmed Milk

4 Teaspoons Baking Powder

$\frac{1}{4}$ Teaspoon Ground Nutmeg

Method: Beat egg whites well. Beat in sugar and oil. Stir in milk.

Sift together flour, baking powder, salt, nutmeg and cinnamon and add to egg mixture. More flour may be added if necessary.

Roll out on floured board, cut into shapes with doughnut cutter. Fry in deep hot oil. Drain and roll in sugar.

✱ CRUMPETS

2 Tablespoons Sugar
1 Tablespoon Sunflower or
    Corn Oil
1 Egg White

About ½ cup Skimmed Milk
1 Cup Flour
2 Teaspoons Baking Powder
    Pinch of Salt

Method: Beat sugar, oil and egg together well. Sift flour, baking powder and salt together and add to sugar mixture, mixing well. Add milk gradually. Mixture must be neither too thick nor too thin.

Drop spoonfuls onto hot oiled hotplate or frying pan. When bubbles appear, turn onto other side.

✱ SHORTCRUST PASTRY (for 8 or 9-inch piedish)

1 Cup Flour
2 Teaspoons Baking Powder
4 Tablespoons Sunflower or Corn Oil

2 Tablespoons Sugar
    Pinch of Salt
1 Egg White

Method: Sift flour, baking powder, salt and sugar together.

Add oil and mix well. Beat in egg white well. (If necessary, add a little iced water.)

Roll between 2 sheets of greaseproof paper, lightly flouring bottom sheet. Remove paper and place in oiled piedish. Prick with fork and bake at 425° for 10-15 minutes.

This pastry can be baked with or without filling and can also be used for stuffed monkeys and other biscuits.

✱ ONE CRUST PIE (A)

1 Cup Sifted Flour
¼ Cup Sunflower or Corn Oil

½ Teaspoon Salt
2 or 3 Tablespoons cold Water

Method: Sift together flour and salt. Add oil and mix until it resembles breadcrumbs.

Sprinkle cold water (one spoon at a time) over mixture, tossing lightly with fork until dough is moist enough to hold together.

Form into ball. Roll out on floured board about 1-2 inches larger than the piedish you are going to use.

Fit pastry loosely into piedish. Gently pat out air pockets and prick with fork. Fold edge to form standing rim and flute same. Bake with or without filling.

If baked without filling, bake in hot oven (450°) for 10-15 minutes.

✱ PASTRY (B) (Two Crust Pie for meats)

5 Tablespoons Sunflower or Corn Oil   ½ Cup Boiling Water
½ lb. Self-raising Flour   ¼ Teaspoon Salt

Method: Mix oil with boiling water, add salt. Stir in flour gradually, mixing well until dough is hard enough and comes away from mixing bowl clean. Chill in refrigerator for about 1 hour. Roll out once on floured board.

Wrap in greasproof paper and return to refrigerator until required.

This can be kept for 3-4 days.

✱ TWO CRUST PIE (C)

2 Cups Flour   1 Level Teaspoon Salt
½ Cup Sunflower or Corn Oil   4-5 Tablespoons Cold Water

Method: Sift together flour and salt. Add oil and mix until it resembles coarse breadcrumbs. Sprinkle water (1 tablespoonful at a time) over mixture, tossing lightly with a fork until dough is moist enough to hold together.

Divide dough in half and form into two balls. Roll out on floured board two circles (about 2 inches larger than piedish).

Fit one circle of pastry loosely into piedish. Gently pat out air pockets and prick with a fork.

Fill with desired filling and cover with remaining circle of pastry.

Fold edge of top pastry under lower pastry to form a standing rim. Flute with thumb and fingers. Cut slits on top of pastry to allow steam to escape.

✳ BASIC PASTRY FOR BISCUITS AND TARTS

¾ Cup Sugar
2 Beaten Egg Whites
  Almost 1 lb. Self-raising Flour
  Pinch of Salt

8 Tablespoons Sunflower or
  Corn Oil
1 Teaspoon Vanilla Essence
1 Teaspoon Baking Powder

Method: Mix oil and sugar together. Add beaten egg whites and vanilla essence and mix well. Fold in half the flour, sifted with baking powder and salt, then gradually add more sifted flour, mixing well, until pastry comes away from bowl clean. This is rather a sticky dough.

Wrap dough in greaseproof paper and place in refrigerator for at least 3 hours. This pastry can be kept for about 2 weeks. Cut off pieces and use as required.

For Tarts:
Place pastry between two pieces of greaseproof paper, flouring bottom sheet. Roll out to size required. Remove top sheet of paper and, holding bottom sheet, place on piedish. Remove paper and prick pastry.

Bake in oiled and floured dish at 350° for about 10 minutes.

For Biscuits:
Place pastry on floured board, cover with greaseproof paper and roll out to about ⅛ inch thickness. Remove paper and cut into shapes required. Bake on ungreased baking sheet at 350° for 7-10 minutes.

✳ ALMOND TART

1 Cup Ground Almonds
1 Cup Sugar
  Pinch of Salt
1 Egg White
1 Cup Flour (sifted)

1 Teaspoon Baking Powder
4 Tablespoons Sunflower or
  Corn Oil
1 Tablespoon Malt Vinegar

Method: Mix Almonds, flour, sugar, baking powder, salt and oil together.

Bind with egg white and vinegar and mix well. (This is a soft pastry.)

Make into balls and divide in two. Line two 7- or 8-inch sandwich tins with greaseproof paper and oil. Press pastry into each tin lightly with floured fingers.

Bake in oven 325° for 25-30 minutes.

(The pastry will still be soft but will harden when cold.)

Sandwich together with a filling of apricot jam when cold.

✱ CHEESE TART

Pastry:

1 Tablespoon Sunflower or Corn Oil
Pinch of Salt
1½ Tablespoons Skimmed Milk

A little Apricot Jam
1 Tablespoon Sugar
¾ Cup Self-raising Flour

Filling:

¾ lb. Skim Milk Cheese
2 Tablespoons Sugar
½ Teaspoon Vanilla Essence
2 Egg Whites

1 Tablespoon Cinnamon
2 Tablespoons Skimmed Milk
¼ Cup Seedless Raisins (optional)
Pinch of Salt

Method—Pastry:

Mix oil, salt, sugar, milk together and gradually add sifted flour to make a firm dough. Form into smooth ball between cupped hands and roll out on floured board to size of piedish. Oil piedish and line with pastry. Prick with fork, line with a little apricot jam and add filling.

Bake at 375° for 30 minutes.

Filling:

Beat 2 egg whites very stiffly. Mix cheese, sugar, vanilla essence, salt, cinnamon, milk and raisins together and then fold in the egg whites. Fill the pastry shell.

* MILK TART

Shortcrust Pastry (see on
   page 87
2 Level Tablespoons Custard
   Powder
½ Teaspoon Ground Nutmeg
1 Teaspoon Ground Cinnamon

½ Pint Skimmed Milk and a
   little extra
1 Teaspoon Vanilla Essence
1 Tablespoon Sugar
2 Well beaten Egg Whites

Method: Roll out shortcrust pastry very thinly and bake for half
the time stipulated. Leave to get cold.

Bring the ½ pint milk to the boil. Meanwhile, mix custard
powder with a little extra milk to make a soft paste. Add vanilla
essence and nutmeg. When milk comes to the boil, stir in the
custard powder mixture until same thickens.

Remove from stove and beat well until custard is light and
frothy. Then fold in well beaten egg whites and mix well.

Pour into baked pastry shell.

Mix sugar and cinnamon together and sprinkle on top of
custard filling. Bake at 250° for ½ to ¾ hour.

Remove from oven and allow to cool, when it will sink
gradually to the level of the piedish.

* SWISS TART

2 Cups Flour
2 Teaspoons Baking Powder
½ Teaspoon Vanilla Essence
½ Teaspoon Malt Vinegar

½ Cup Sugar
4 Tablespoons Sunflower or
   Corn Oil
1 Egg White

Method: Mix oil and sugar well. Beat egg white, vinegar and
vanilla essence together and add to oil mixture. Add sifted
baking powder and flour. Mix well.

With fingers, press half or more pastry evenly and firmly into
an oiled piedish, then press up sides. Prick surface with fork.
Add jam or any other filling, and cover by crumbling balance of
pastry over the top.

Bake for 45 minutes in medium oven (350°-375°).

✱ SKIM MILK CHEESE AND APPLE FILLING

½ lb. Skim Milk Cheese
½ Teaspoon Ground Nutmeg
1 Tablespoon Cornflour
1 Tablespoon Skimmed Milk
   Apricot Jam

1 Sour Apple, roughly grated
1 Teaspoon Ground Cinnamon
1 Tablespoon Lemon Juice
2 Tablespoons Sugar or more
    to taste

Method: Use shortcrust pastry, page 87.

Mix cheese and grated apple with lemon juice. Add cinnamon, nutmeg, sugar and cornflour. Mix well.

Prick piecrust and spread a little apricot jam evenly over same. Add cheese mixture and bake at 425° for 15-20 minutes.

✱ ORANGE FILLING

3 Slightly heaped Tablespoons Flour
1 Cup Orange Juice
2 Tablespoons Sunflower or
   Corn Oil

½ Cup Sugar
1½ Tablespoons Lemon
   Juice

Method: Combine and mix thoroughly the above ingredients. Cook over low heat, stirring constantly until mixture begins to boil and thicken.

Remove from heat.

Delicious as filling for sandwich cakes or over apple tart.

✱ PINEAPPLE FILLING

¼ Cup Cornflour
¾ Cup hot Water
2 Teaspoons Lemon Juice

½ Cup Sugar
1 Cup Crushed Pineapple (tinned)

Method: Blend together cornflour and sugar. Add hot water gradually.

Cook until thick and clear, stirring constantly.

Add crushed pineapple and lemon juice. Cool.

✻ FRUIT FILLING FOR TART

½ Cup Saltanas
¼ Cup Seedless Currants
1 Teaspoon Ground Cinnamon

¼ Cup Seedless Raisins
1 Tablespoon Sugar
1 Tablespoon Brandy

Method: Mix all above together. Prick base of pastry and line with apricot jam and then add fruit mixture.

✻ PINEAPPLE AND CUSTARD FILLING FOR TART

2 Pineapples, peeled and finely
   grated
4 Teaspoons Sugar, or more, to
   taste

1 Level Tablespoon Custard
   Powder

Method: Mix all ingredients well together and fill into baked piecrust. Bake at 350° for 20-30 minutes.

BISCUITS

Biscuits made with oil improve if kept for a few days. Store in an airtight tin.

* RICE KRISPIE BISCUITS

1 Level Tablespoon Sunflower or Corn Oil
4 Level Tablespoons Golden Syrup

1 Level Tablespoon Sugar
3 oz. Rice Krispies
½ Teaspoon Vanilla Essence

Method: Melt oil, sugar and Golden Syrup in a medium-sized saucepan.

Stir with wooden spoon and boil for 1 minute, i.e. until sugar has completely melted. Remove from stove, add flavouring and stir in Rice Krispies. Mix thoroughly.

Turn out onto a board or flat biscuit tin, cover with wax paper and roll out until flat and about ¼ inch thick. Remove paper and leave to cool. When cold, cut in squares.

* RICE KRISPIES AND NUT BISCUITS

2 Egg Whites
Pinch of Salt
¾ Cup Castor Sugar

2 Cups Rice Krispies
2 Cups Shelled Peanuts
½ Teaspoon Vanilla Essence

Method: Beat egg whites with salt until very stiff. Add castor sugar gradually (about 1 dessertspoon at a time) and continue beating until mixture holds its shape. Fold in Rice Krispies and peanuts and finally add the flavouring.

Drop teaspoonful of the mixture onto an oiled baking sheet and bake at 325° for 10-15 minutes.

Allow biscuits to cool slightly before trying to remove from the baking sheet.

* PEANUT BUTTER BISCUITS

2½ Cups Flour
1 Teaspoon Bicarbonate of Soda
8 Tablespoons Sunflower or
   Corn Oil
1 Teaspoon Almond Essence

1 Teaspoon Baking Powder
1 Cup Sugar
   Pinch of Salt
2 Egg Whites
½ lb. Peanut Butter

Method: Sift all dry ingredients together. Add oil and mix well. Mix in well beaten egg whites and almond essence. Lastly add peanut butter and blend well to make a stiff dough.

Make into balls, the size of a small marble and press slightly between the palms of your hands. Place on ungreased biscuit tin and press down with fork.

Bake in moderate oven at 350° for 10-15 minutes.

* RICE KRISPIE CRUNCHIES

7 Cups Rice Krispies
3 Tablespoons Oil

25 Marshmallows

Method: Melt marshmallows and oil very gently, stirring continually.

When melted, remove from stove and add Rice Krispies, mixing thoroughly. Turn out onto ungreased baking sheet pressing and packing same well, about ¾ inch thick.

Leave to get cold, then cut into squares.

* ALMOND MACAROONS

3 Egg Whites
½ lb. Shredded Almonds
2 Heaped Tablespoons Matzo Meal*

1 Cup Sugar
1 Teaspoon Lemon
   Juice

Method: Beat egg whites very stiff, then beat in sugar slowly.

Mix in almonds and lemon juice. Lastly, add matzo meal to make a stiff mixture.

Line baking sheet with greaseproof paper and oil paper well.

Put teaspoonfuls of mixture onto same and bake at 375° for 15-20 minutes until slightly brown.

* Matzo Meal can be obtained at Health Food Stores.

✳ CORNFLAKE BISCUITS

1 Cup Flour
1 Egg White
  Pinch of Salt
1 Tablespoon Sunflower or
  Corn Oil
¾ Cup Raisins and Currants
  mixed

1 oz Cut-up Walnuts
1 Teaspoon Baking Powder
½ Teaspoon Vanilla Essence
½ Cup of Sugar
1½ Tablespoons Skimmed
  Milk
Crushed Cornflakes

Method: Mix dry ingredients, add in oil and beaten egg white. Mix well. Add milk and essence. Mixture must not be hard.

Now add raisins and currants and walnuts. Roll teaspoonfuls of dough into the crushed cornflakes making into small balls. Place on oiled baking sheet, 2 inches apart.

Bake in moderate oven (350°) for 30-35 minutes, or until slightly browned.

✳ CORNFLAKE MACAROONS

2 Egg Whites
  Pinch of Salt
1 Cup Sugar
1 Cup Dates (chopped finely)

½ Teaspoon Vanilla Essence
2 Cups Cornflakes
1 Cup Shelled Peanuts
1 Cup Sultanas

Method: Beat egg whites with salt until very stiff. Mix the rest of the ingredients together and fold into egg mixture.

Drop teaspoonfuls of the mixture onto an oiled, waxed paper-lined baking sheet and bake in a moderate oven (350°) for 15-20 minutes.

Allow biscuits to cool slightly before trying to remove from baking sheet.

✳ CINNAMON BISCUITS

1 Cup Sunflower or Corn Oil
1 Egg White (unbeaten)
1 Tablespoon Skimmed Milk
1 lb. Self-raising Flour (or less)

¾ Cup Sugar
1 Teaspoon Malt Vinegar
1 Teaspoon Vanilla Essence

Method: Mix all the ingredients (except the flour) well together. Add the flour gradually to make a firm dough. Form into smooth ball between floured cupped hands, place on floured board, cover with greaseproof paper and roll. Remove paper. Cut into shapes with biscuit cutter.

Dip into cinnamon and sugar mixture (in the proportion of $\frac{1}{2}$ teaspoon cinnamon to about 1 tablespoon sugar).

(*Note:* The amount of sugar stated in ingredients does not include the sugar used to make the cinnamon and sugar mixture.)

Bake on ungreased baking sheet at 375° for 15-20 minutes.

✱ CRISPY BISCUITS

4 Tablespoons Sunflower or Corn Oil	4 oz. Castor Sugar
8 oz. Sifted Flour	$\frac{1}{2}$ Teaspoon Strawberry Essence
1 Level Teaspoon Baking Powder	1 Egg White
	1 Tablespoon cold Water

Method: Mix oil and sugar very well, mix in flour with hands.

Add essence and egg white, mix to a stiff paste with the water.

Roll out on slightly floured board to $\frac{1}{4}$ inch thickness. Prick the surface with a fork and cut into required shapes with cutter. Oil baking sheets and bake in oven (375°) for 10-15 minutes.

These biscuits can also be made into jam or orange rings by cutting the dough in rounds with a 2-inch cutter. Remove and discard the centre of half the rounds with a 1-inch cutter, making rings. Bake the whole round on one baking sheet and the rings on another baking sheet. When the biscuits are cool, spread the rounds with jam or orange filling (see Fillings).

Place a ring on each round, putting extra filling in the centre.

✱ RUM AND COFFEE SQUARES

$1\frac{3}{4}$ Cups Flour	$\frac{1}{2}$ Teaspoon Baking Powder
$\frac{1}{2}$ Teaspoon Salt	$\frac{1}{2}$ Teaspoon Bicarbonate of Soda
$\frac{1}{2}$ Cup Sugar	5 Tablespoons Sunflower or Corn Oil
1 Egg White	
1 Teaspoon Rum Essence	2 Tablespoons Skimmed Milk
Apricot Jam	1 Teaspoon Coffee Essence

Method: Sift together flour, baking powder, salt, bicarbonate of soda and sugar. Mix in oil until mixture looks like fine breadcrumbs. Blend in egg white and milk. Mix until smooth. Divide dough in half. Add rum essence to one half and the coffee essence to the other half. With floured fingers knead each half separately until essences are well blended with dough. Roll out one half on floured board to ⅛ inch thickness. Cut into squares with a 2-inch by 2-inch cutter. Place on an oiled baking sheet.

Repeat this procedure with the other half, placing same on another baking sheet. Bake in moderate oven (375°) for 5-10 minutes. When biscuits are cold, sandwich rum and coffee biscuit together with apricot jam.

✱ CHERRY BISCUITS

½ Cup Sunflower or Corn Oil
3 Egg Whites
1 lb. Self-raising Flour (sifted)
   Cherries—cut in quarters
1 Cup Sugar
1 Teaspoon Malt Vinegar
1 Teaspoon Orange Essence

Method: Heat oil (do not allow to boil), beat in sugar and leave to cool.

Add egg whites, one at a time, beating well after each and add vinegar. Now add flour, mixing well. Lastly add essence.

Make into small balls about the size of a shilling, and place on oiled baking sheet. Press flat with fork and place a quarter cherry in centre of each. Bake at 375° for 10-15 minutes.

✱ GARIBALDI BISCUITS

4 oz. Self-raising Flour
1 Tablespoon Sunflower or
   Corn Oil
2 oz. Currants (cleaned)
2 Tablespoons Skimmed Milk
   Pinch of Salt
1 oz. Sugar
1 Dessertspoon Vinegar

Method: Sift flour and salt into mixing bowl. Mix in oil lightly. Add sugar and vinegar. Mix to a fairly stiff dough with about 1½ tablespoons milk.

Turn onto a lightly floured board and roll out evenly to a square about ⅛ inch thick. Prick the square and cut in half.

Sprinkle one half with the currants and cover with the other half. Re-flour the board and roll out the dough again to same thickness as before, keeping it a good square shape. Trim edges and cut into 2-inch squares. Deeply mark the squares diagonally with a knife. Brush with the remaining milk and place on an oiled baking sheet.

Bake in oven (400°) for 15-20 minutes.

Cool and break into triangles.

* SWEET BISCUIT

4 Egg Whites
¾ Cup Sunflower or Corn Oil
  Pinch of Salt
1 lb. Self-raising Flour

1 Teaspoon Malt Vinegar
¾ Cup Sugar
1 Teaspoon grated Lemon
  Rind

Method: Mix sugar, egg and vinegar very well, add oil, salt and lemon rind and mix. Lastly add flour to make firm dough. Roll out very thin on floured board. Cut into shapes, place on oiled baking sheets, and bake on lowest shelf of oven (375°) for 7-10 minutes.

* OAT BISCUITS

1 Cup Flour
1 Cup Breakfast Oats
1 Teaspoon Bicarbonate of Soda
1 Heaped Tablespoon Golden
  Syrup
1 Teaspoon Vanilla Essence

½ Cup Sugar
½ Cup Ground Almonds
1 Tablespoon Boiling Water
4 Tablespoons Sunflower or
  Corn Oil

Method: Sift flour and sugar together. Add oats and ground almonds. Dissolve bicarbonate of soda in boiling water. Boil together oil and golden syrup. Make a hole in centre of flour mixture and add boiling oil mixture and the dissolved bicarbonate of soda. Now mix all together well with a spoon.

Mix in essence. This is a crumbly dough. Press one dessertspoon-full at a time into flat rounds with fingers. Place on oiled baking sheet and bake in oven (400°) for 10-15 minutes until brown.

* COFFEE SANDWICH FINGERS

1¾ Cups Flour	½ Teaspoon Baking Powder
½ Teaspoon Salt	½ Teaspoon Bicarbonate of Soda
½ Cup Sugar	5 Tablespoons Sunflower or
1 Egg White	Corn Oil
1 Teaspoon Vanilla Essence	2 Tablespoons Skimmed Milk
Apricot Jam	2 Teaspoons Instant Coffee

Method: Sift together flour, baking powder, salt, bicarbonate of soda, and sugar. Mix in oil until mixture resembles fine bread-crumbs. Add egg white. Mix together instant coffee and milk and add into mixture. Add essence. Knead with fingers until well blended and smooth. Roll out on floured board to ⅛ inch thick-ness. Cut into fingers 2½ inches long and 1 inch wide.

Place on oiled baking sheet, and bake in moderate oven (375°) for 7-10 minutes. When cold, sandwich biscuits together with jam.

* ORANGE BISCUITS

4 Tablespoons Sunflower or	1 Tablespoon Orange Juice
Corn Oil	5 oz. Sugar
½ Teaspoon Salt	1 Egg White
1 Heaped Teaspoon Orange	7 oz. Flour
Rind	½ Teaspoon Bicarbonate of Soda

Method: Mix oil and sugar, blend in egg white, orange juice and orange rind and beat very well. Add sifted flour and bicarbonate of soda, making a soft dough. Form into a roll, 1½ inches in diameter and roll up in greaseproof paper, screw up ends lightly and place in refrigerator for at least two hours, and then slice into rounds of ¼ inch thickness. Place on oiled baking sheets, a short distance apart, as they spread, put a quartered cherry or nut on top of each and bake in oven at 400° for 10-15 minutes.

✳ FRUIT BISCUITS

1 Cup Sunflower or Corn Oil	¾ Cup Sugar
1 Egg White (unbeaten)	1 Tablespoon Skimmed Milk
1 Teaspoon Vanilla Essence	1 lb. Self-raising Flour (or less)
1 Teaspoon Malt Vinegar	

Method: Mix oil, sugar, egg, vinegar, milk and essence together.

Add flour gradually and mix to make firm dough. Take half of the pastry and roll out between two sheets of waxed paper, the size of the baking sheet.

Remove top sheet of paper and turn bottom sheet upside down in exact position wanted over baking sheet and remove paper. Fill dough with fruit mixture. Roll out balance of pastry in the same way and cover fruit mixture. Prick entire surface. Bake for 20-25 minutes, or until golden brown in moderate oven (375°).

While hot, cut in squares.

Fruit Mixture:

1 Cup mixed Cake Fruit	1 Tablespoon Sugar
1 Dessertspoon Cinnamon	1 Tablespoon Brandy

Mix all together.

✳ DIGESTIVE BISCUITS

4 Tablespoons Sunflower or Corn Oil	½ Teaspoon Baking Powder
4 oz. Sugar	12 oz. Brown Flour
1 Egg White (unbeaten)	4 oz. Oatmeal
¼ Cup Skimmed Milk (approx.)	½ Teaspoon Bicarbonate of Soda

Method: Mix oil and sugar well. Beat in egg white. Blend in thoroughly flour, oatmeal, bicarbonate of soda and baking powder.

Add in gradually milk to make a firm dough.

Roll out on slightly floured board and cut into rounds with 2-inch cutter.

Bake on oiled baking sheets in oven (400°) for 10-15 minutes.

✱ EDA'S STUFFED MONKEYS

3½ Cups Flour
3 Heaped Teaspoons Baking Powder
9 Tablespoons Sunflower or
    Corn Oil

¼ Cup Skimmed Milk
¾ Cup Sugar
    Pinch of Salt
3 Egg Whites

Method: Sift flour, sugar, baking powder and salt together. Make hole in centre of flour mixture and add oil, egg whites and milk. Knead well with fingers. If necessary, add a little more flour until dough comes away from bowl clean. Dough must be soft. Divide dough into 4 or 5 pieces. Roll out each piece of dough to about ¼ inch thick on floured board, and fill each piece with filling, as below:

Filling:
3 oz. Currants
3 oz. Mixed Candied Peel
      Mix above together (or 1 lb. mixed cake fruit).

6 oz. Raisins
4 oz. Sultanas

½ Teaspoon Cinnamon, mixed with 1 tablespoon Sugar
  Apricot Jam

Spread dough evenly with a little jam, then sprinkle on mixture of cinnamon and sugar and then the mixed fruits. Roll up into strips slightly smaller than your baking sheet. Place on oiled baking sheet, about 2-3 inches apart and brush tops with milk. Bake in oven (425°) for about 15-20 minutes. Cut into diagonal pieces when cold.

✱ STUFFED MONKEYS

6 Tablespoons Sunflower or
    Corn Oil
2 Cups Flour
2 Egg Whites

    Apricot Jam
4 Teaspoons Baking Powder
3 Tablespoons Sugar
¼ Teaspoon Salt

Method: Sift all dry ingredients together in bowl, add oil and mix well with fork to resemble coarse breadcrumbs. Add beaten egg whites. If necessary, add a little iced water. Dough must be firm. Cut off pieces sufficient to roll into strips of about 5 inches wide and the length of your baking sheet. Roll between two sheets of waxed paper, having lightly floured bottom sheet. When desired width and length is reached, remove top sheet of paper and trim ends of pastry. Spread apricot jam evenly on pastry and fill centre with fruit mixture given below.

Holding the waxed paper, fold one side to centre of fruit filling, removing that side of paper when this is done. Do the same with the other side, only this must fold over the other side of the pastry. Lift the strips onto your baking sheet and prick with fork. Repeat until all the dough has been used. Bake in oven (425°) for 15-20 minutes.

Leave to cool and then cut diagonally about 1½ to 2 inches wide.

Filling:

½ lb. Mixed Cake Fruit
½ Teaspoon Nutmeg
1½ Tablespoons Brandy (optional)

2 Teaspoons Cinnamon
4 Teaspoons Sugar

Mix all together.

✱ RAISIN FILLED COOKIES

1¾ Cups Flour
½ Teaspoon Salt
½ Cup Sugar
1 Egg White
1 Teaspoon Vanilla Essence

½ Teaspoon Baking Powder
½ Teaspoon Bicarbonate of Soda
5 Tablespoons Sunflower or
    Corn Oil
2 Tablespoons Skimmed Milk

Method: Sift together flour, baking powder, salt, bicarbonate of soda, and sugar. Mix in oil until mixture looks like fine breadcrumbs. Blend in egg white, milk and vanilla essence and mix until smooth. Roll out on floured board to ⅛ inch thickness. Cut into rounds with 2½-inch cutter. Fill centre of half the rounds with 1 teaspoon of the following raisin mixture and cover with the remaining rounds. Seal edges with fork and prick top.

Bake in moderate oven 375° for 10-15 minutes.

Filling:

1½ Cups chopped Raisins
½ Cup Water
1 Tablespoon Lemon Juice

½ Cup Sugar
½ Teaspoon Lemon Rind
¼ Cup chopped Nuts

Mix raisins, sugar and water in saucepan. Cook for 15 minutes, or until thick, stirring constantly. Remove from heat. Mix in lemon rind, lemon juice and nuts. Fill cookies as directed above.

✱ GINGER BISCUITS

4 Egg Whites
1 lb. Tin Golden Syrup
2 Level Tablespoons Mixed Spice
½ Cup Sunflower or Corn Oil
1 Teaspoon Bicarbonate of Soda
1 Cup Currants, Sultanas and Lemon
    Peel (optional)

1 Tablespoon Vinegar
5 Cups Flour
1½ Cups Sugar
1 Teaspoon Baking Powder
1 Level Tablespoon
    Ground Ginger
1 Tot Brandy

Method: Beat egg whites and vinegar and sugar well. Add syrup and oil. Sift all dry ingredients, add fruit, then add all into egg mixture to form a fairly stiff dough. Add brandy, mixing well all the time.

Turn into two baking tins (14 by 10 inches) and bake in a slow oven (300°) for about two hours.

Cut into diamond shapes when cold.

✱ GINGER STRIPS

2 Egg Whites
1 Teaspoon Malt Vinegar
1 Cup Brown Sugar
1 Cup Golden Syrup
1 Cup Sunflower or
    Corn Oil
2 Teaspoons Bicarbonate of
    Soda

¼ Teaspoon Salt
2 Teaspoons Ginger
2 Teaspoons Mixed Spice
1½ Teaspoons Ground Cinnamon
5 Cups Flour
½ Teaspoon Ground Cloves

Method: Beat together egg whites, vinegar, syrup and oil for two minutes.

Sift dry ingredients together and add to egg white mixture, gradually, mixing well to make a soft dough. Extra cup of sifted flour may be added if necessary. Roll into strips with hands, about 1 inch in diameter, the length of baking sheet. Press down with hand to about $\frac{1}{2}$ inch thick and 2 inches wide. Place each strip about $1\frac{1}{2}$ inches apart to allow for spreading. Oil baking sheet and bake in oven at 350° for 25-30 minutes.

Leave to cool for 5 minutes then cut into diagonal pieces.

✳ GINGER STUFFED MONKEYS

4 Tablespoons Sunflower or Corn Oil	2 Egg Whites
	1 Teaspoon Malt Vinegar
1 Teaspoon Bicarbonate of Soda	1 Teaspoon Ground Cinnamon
$\frac{1}{2}$ Teaspoon Ground Nutmeg	1 Tablespoon Ground Ginger
2 Tablespoons Golden Syrup	$3\frac{1}{2}$-4 Cups Flour (sifted)
4 Level Tablespoons Sugar	

Method: Mix oil and sugar together. Add all the other ingredients, except the flour. Add flour gradually to make soft dough which comes away from bowl clean. Divide dough into about 5 pieces.

Filling:

$\frac{1}{2}$ lb. Prunes (remove pips)	$\frac{1}{2}$ lb. Seedless Raisins
$\frac{1}{2}$ lb. Sultanas	$\frac{1}{4}$ lb. Mixed Peel
2 oz. Preserved Ginger, cut up (optional)	2 Tablespoons Apricot Jam

Mince prunes, raisins and sultanas together. Then mix in jam to soften fruit. Roll out one piece of dough on a floured board about 5 inches wide and a little shorter than the length of baking sheet to be used and about $\frac{1}{4}$ inch thick. Spread this thickly with the minced fruit, then sprinkle with the mixed peel and cut up preserved ginger. Roll up dough with hands to make strips of about $1\frac{1}{2}$ inches wide. Close up ends by pinching together with fingers to keep filling in. Repeat procedure with the remaining pieces of dough. Place strips on oiled baking tin about 1 inch apart and brush tops with egg white *or* skimmed milk and sprinkle with sugar. Bake in oven at 350° for 20-25 minutes. Cut into pieces diagonally when cold.

✱ MILK SCONES

½ lb. Flour
4 Teaspoons Baking Powder
¾ Cup Skimmed Milk

½ Teaspoon Salt
2 Tablespoons Sunflower or
    Corn Oil

Method: Sift dry ingredients and mix oil into flour mixture. Add milk and stir to make a soft dough. Turn onto floured board and toss with floured hands until smooth. Pat out to ¾ inch thick, cut into rounds or any desired shape.

    Place on greased baking sheet and bake in hot oven (450°) for 10-12 minutes.

✱ SWEET SCONES

2 Cups Flour
1 Egg White
¼ Cup Sugar
2¼ Teaspoons Sunflower or
    Corn Oil

2 Teaspoons Baking Powder
½ Teaspoon Salt
1 Teaspoon Vanilla Essence
½ Cup Skimmed Milk (or more)

Method: Mix all dry ingredients, then add oil and mix well. Beat eggs well and add to flour mixture. Then add milk.

    Consistency must not be hard, but must not stick to board. Flour board, and flatten dough with palms of hands about ½ inch thick. Cut into shape and brush tops of scones with milk. Place on oiled baking sheet and bake in oven at 400° for 10-15 minutes.

✱ PLAIN SCONES

8 oz. Flour
3 Level Teaspoons Baking Powder
1 oz. Castor Sugar
½ Level Teaspoon Salt

2 Tablespoons Sunflower or
    Corn Oil
6 Tablespoons Skimmed Milk

Method: Sift flour, salt and baking powder into mixing bowl. Add oil and mix with fingers until the mixture resembles fine breadcrumbs. Mix in sugar.

Add the milk and mix to a soft dough. Turn dough onto a lightly floured board and knead with floured fingers until the dough is smooth. Roll out to a round, $\frac{1}{4}$ inch thick. Cut into rounds with a 2-inch cutter. Re-roll remaining pieces of dough and cut into similar rounds.

Place scones on an oiled baking sheet and brush tops with milk.

Bake in oven at 425° for 10 minutes.

✱ CURRANT SCONES

8 oz. Self-raising Flour
1 Level Teaspoon Baking Powder
2 oz. Castor Sugar
1 Egg White (beaten)
3½ Tablespoons Skimmed Milk

½ Level Teaspoon Salt
2 Tablespoons Sunflower or Corn Oil
3 oz. Currants (washed and dried)

Method: Sift flour, salt and baking powder into a mixing bowl. Add oil and mix until mixture resembles fine breadcrumbs. Add in the sugar and currants and mix to a soft dough with the beaten egg white and milk. Turn the dough onto a slightly floured board and knead quickly with floured hands.

Roll the dough out to a round $\frac{1}{2}$ inch thick. Cut with 2-inch cutter. Re-roll remaining pieces of dough and cut into similar rounds.

Place scones on an oiled baking sheet and brush tops with milk. Bake in oven at 425° for 20-25 minutes.

✱ MIXED FRUIT SCONES

8 oz. Self-raising Flour
2 Tablespoons Sunflower or Corn Oil
2 oz. Mixed Cake Fruit

Pinch of Salt
1 Level Tablespoon Castor Sugar
5 Tablespoons Skimmed Milk

Method: Sift flour and salt into a bowl, and mix in the oil until it looks like fine breadcrumbs. Add sugar and mixed fruits. Mix to a stiff dough with milk.

Place the dough on a floured board and knead until smooth. Roll out to $\frac{1}{2}$ inch thick and cut with 2-inch cutter into rounds. Place rounds on oiled baking sheet and put into oven (450°) for 7-10 minutes or until well risen and slightly brown.

✳ CHEESE SCONES

1 Cup Flour (sifted)
2 Teaspoons Baking Powder
1 Cup Skimmed Milk

1 Cup Finely Grated Yellow
  Skim Milk Cheese
Salt and Pepper

Method: Mix flour and cheese together. Add milk, mixing well. Add salt and pepper to taste. Lastly, add baking powder. Mix very well. This is a softish mixture.

Oil Muffin tins and with tablespoon half fill each. Bake at 350°-400° for 10-15 minutes. Makes 12 large muffins.

Mix skim milk cheese with a little dry mustard, cayenne pepper and salt to taste and moisten with skimmed milk.

Chopped up pickled cucumber may be added.

*

Mix together well, skim milk cheese with sardine or Anchovette paste and chopped up cucumber or lettuce.

*

Mix skim milk cheese with honey or golden syrup and mashed bananas.

*

Mix skim milk cheese with Piccalilli.

*

Mix stoneless dates, mashed with a little lemon or orange juice.

*

Mash bananas and dates with a little lemon juice and mix in chopped nuts.

*

Mash an avocado pear and mix with a little salt, pepper and lemon juice.

*

Mix together:

¼ lb. Skim Milk Cheese	1 Teaspoon Sunflower or
1 Egg White	Corn Oil
½ Teaspoon Dry Mustard	1 Teaspoon Vinegar

Cook on low heat for 5-10 minutes until it comes to the boil, stirring constantly. Add cayenne pepper and salt to taste.

This can be served as a warm savoury on toast, or cold as a spread.

INDEX